P9-DIA-865

AGAINST MARRIAGE

THE
OTHER VOICE
IN
EARLY MODERN
EUROPE

A Series Edited by Margaret L. King and Albert Rabil Jr.

OTHER BOOKS IN THE SERIES

Anne-Marie-Louise d'Orléans
Duchesse de Montpensier

AGAINST MARRIAGE

The Correspondence of
La Grande Mademoiselle

ॐ

Edited and Translated
by
Joan DeJean

THE UNIVERSITY OF CHICAGO PRESS
Chicago & London

Anne-Marie-Louise d'Orléans, duchesse de Montpensier, 1627–1693

Joan DeJean is Trustee Professor of French at the University of Pennsylvania. Her previous books include *Fictions of Sappho, 1546–1937; Tender Geographies: Women and the Origins of the Novel in France; Ancients against Moderns: Culture Wars and the Making of a Fin de Siècle;* and *The Reinvention of Obscenity: Sex, Lies, and Tabloids in Early Modern France.*

The University of Chicago Press, Chicago 60637
The University of Chicago Press, Ltd., London
© 2002 by The University of Chicago
All rights reserved. Published 2002
Printed in the United States of America
11 10 09 08 07 06 05 04 03 02   1 2 3 4 5

Library of Congress Cataloging-in-Publication Data

Montpensier, Anne-Marie-Louise d'Orléans, duchesse de, 1627–1693.
[Correspondence. English & French]
Against marriage : the correspondence of la Grande Mademoiselle / edited and translated by Joan DeJean.
    p. cm.—(The other voice in early modern Europe)
Includes bibliographical references and index.
Text in English and French.
ISBN 0-226-53490-1 (cloth : alk. paper)—ISBN 0-226-53492-8 (pbk. : alk. paper)
1. Montpensier, Anne-Marie-Louise d'Orléans, duchesse de, 1627–1693—
Correspondence. 2. Motteville, Françoise de, d. 1689—Correspondence.
3. Princesses—France—Correspondence. 4. Ladies-in-waiting—France—
Correspondence. 5. France—History—Louis XIV, 1643–1715. 6. France—
Court and courtiers—History—17th century. 7. Marriage. 8. Sex role.
I. Motteville, Françoise de, d. 1689. II. DeJean, Joan E. III. Title. IV. Series.
DC130.M8 A4 2002
944'.033'0922—dc21

2002007082

⊗ The paper used in this publication meets the minimum requirements of the American National Standard for Information Sciences—Permanence of Paper for Printed Library Materials, ANSI Z39.48–1992.

CONTENTS

THE OTHER VOICE IN
EARLY MODERN EUROPE:
INTRODUCTION TO THE SERIES

Margaret L. King and Albert Rabil Jr.

THE OLD VOICE AND THE OTHER VOICE

In western Europe and the United States, women are nearing equality in the professions, in business, and in politics. Most enjoy access to education, reproductive rights, and autonomy in financial affairs. Issues vital to women are on the public agenda: equal pay, childcare, domestic abuse, breast cancer research, and curricular revision with an eye to the inclusion of women.

These recent achievements have their origins in things women (and some male supporters) said for the first time about six hundred years ago. Theirs is the "other voice," in contradistinction to the "first voice," the voice of the educated men who created Western culture. Coincident with a general reshaping of European culture in the period 1300–1700 (called the Renaissance or early modern period), questions of female equality and opportunity were raised that still resound and are still unresolved.

The other voice emerged against the backdrop of a three-thousand-year history of the derogation of women rooted in the civilizations related to Western culture: Hebrew, Greek, Roman, and Christian. Negative attitudes toward women inherited from these traditions pervaded the intellectual, medical, legal, religious, and social systems that developed during the European Middle Ages.

The following pages describe the traditional, overwhelmingly male views of women's nature inherited by early modern Europeans and the new tradition that the other voice called into being to begin to challenge reigning assumptions. This review should serve as a framework for the understanding of the texts published in the series The Other Voice in Early Modern Europe. Introductions specific to each text and author follow this essay in all the volumes of the series.

TRADITIONAL VIEWS OF WOMEN, 500 B.C.E.–1500 C.E.

Embedded in the philosophical and medical theories of the ancient Greeks were perceptions of the female as inferior to the male in both mind and body. Similarly, the structure of civil legislation inherited from the ancient Romans was biased against women, and the views on women developed by Christian thinkers out of the Hebrew Bible and the Christian New Testament were negative and disabling. Literary works composed in the vernacular language of ordinary people, and widely recited or read, conveyed these negative assumptions. The social networks within which most women lived—those of the family and the institutions of the Roman Catholic Church—were shaped by this negative tradition and sharply limited the areas in which women might act in and upon the world.

GREEK PHILOSOPHY AND FEMALE NATURE. Greek biology assumed that women were inferior to men and defined them merely as childbearers and housekeepers. This view was authoritatively expressed in the works of the philosopher Aristotle.

Aristotle thought in dualities. He considered action superior to inaction, form (the inner design or structure of any object) superior to matter, completion superior to incompletion, possession superior to deprivation. In each of these dualities, he associated the male principle with the superior quality and the female with the inferior. "The male principle in nature," he argued, "is associated with active, formative and perfected characteristics, while the female is passive, material and deprived, desiring the male in order to become complete."[1] Men are always identified with virile qualities, such as judgment, courage, and stamina, and women with their opposites— irrationality, cowardice, and weakness.

Even in the womb, the masculine principle was considered superior. The man's semen, Aristotle believed, created the form of a new human creature, while the female body contributed only matter. (The existence of the ovum, and with it the other facts of human embryology, were not established until the seventeenth century.) Although the later Greek physician Galen believed that there was a female component in generation, contributed by "female semen," the followers of both Aristotle and Galen saw the male role in human generation as more active and more important.

---

1. Aristotle, *Physics* 1.9.192a20–24, in *The Complete Works of Aristotle,* ed. Jonathan Barnes, rev. Oxford trans., 2 vols. (Princeton, 1984), 1:328.

In the Aristotelian view, the male principle sought always to reproduce itself. The creation of a female was always a mistake, therefore, resulting from an imperfect act of generation. Every female born was considered a "defective" or "mutilated" male (as Aristotle's terminology has variously been translated), a "monstrosity" of nature.[2]

For Greek theorists, the biology of males and females was the key to their psychology. The female was softer and more docile, more apt to be despondent, querulous, and deceitful. Being incomplete, moreover, she craved sexual fulfillment in intercourse with a male. The male was intellectual, active, and in control of his passions.

These psychological polarities derived from the theory that the universe consisted of four elements (earth, fire, air, and water), expressed in human bodies as four "humors" (black bile, yellow bile, blood, and phlegm) considered respectively dry, hot, damp, and cold and corresponding to mental states ("melancholic," "choleric," "sanguine," "phlegmatic"). In this schematization, the male, sharing the principles of earth and fire, was dry and hot; the female, sharing the principles of air and water, was cold and damp.

Female psychology was further affected by her dominant organ, the uterus (womb), *hystera* in Greek. The passions generated by the womb made women lustful, deceitful, talkative, irrational, indeed—when these affects were in excess—"hysterical."

Aristotle's biology also had social and political consequences. If the male principle was superior and the female inferior, then in the household, as in the state, men should rule and women must be subordinate. That hierarchy does not rule out the companionship of husband and wife, whose cooperation was necessary for the welfare of children and the preservation of property. Such mutuality supported male preeminence.

Aristotle's teacher Plato suggested a different possibility: that men and women might possess the same virtues. The setting for this proposal is the imaginary and ideal Republic that Plato sketches in a dialogue of that name. Here, for a privileged elite capable of leading wisely, all distinctions of class and wealth dissolve, as do, consequently, those of gender. Without households or property, as Plato constructs his ideal society, there is no need for the subordination of women. Women may, therefore, be educated to the same level as men to assume leadership responsibilities. Plato's Republic remained imaginary, however. In real societies, the subordination of women remained the norm and the prescription.

2. Aristotle, *Generation of Animals* 2.3.737a27–28, in *The Complete Works*, 1 : 1144.

The views of women inherited from the Greek philosophical tradition became the basis for medieval thought. In the thirteenth century, the supreme scholastic philosopher Thomas Aquinas, among others, still echoed Aristotle's views of human reproduction, of male and female personalities, and of the preeminent male role in the social hierarchy.

ROMAN LAW AND THE FEMALE CONDITION. Roman law, like Greek philosophy, underlay medieval thought and shaped medieval society. The ancient belief that adult property-owning men should administer households and make decisions affecting the community at large is the very fulcrum of Roman law.

Around 450 B.C.E., during Rome's republican era, the community's customary law was recorded (legendarily) on twelve tablets erected in the city's central forum. It was later elaborated by professional jurists, whose activity increased in the imperial era, when much new legislation, especially on issues affecting family and inheritance, was passed. This growing, changing body of laws was eventually codified in the *Corpus of Civil Law* under the direction of the Emperor Justinian, generations after the empire ceased to be ruled from Rome. That *Corpus,* read and commented on by medieval scholars from the eleventh century on, inspired the legal systems of most of the cities and kingdoms of Europe.

Laws regarding dowries, divorce, and inheritance pertain primarily to women. Since those laws aimed to maintain and preserve property, the women concerned were those from the property-owning minority. Their subordination to male family members points to the even greater subordination of lower-class and slave women, about whom the laws speak little.

In the early republic, the *paterfamilias,* or "father of the family," possessed *patria potestas,* "paternal power." The term *pater,* "father," in both these cases does not necessarily mean biological father but, rather, head of household. The father was the person who owned the household's property and, indeed, its human members. The *paterfamilias* had absolute power—including the power, rarely exercised, of life or death—over his wife, his children, and his slaves, as much as his cattle.

Children could be "emancipated," an act that granted legal autonomy and the right to own property. Male children over fourteen could be emancipated by a special grant from the father or, automatically, by their father's death. But females could never be emancipated; instead, they passed from the authority of their father to a husband or, if widowed or orphaned while still unmarried, to a guardian or tutor.

Marriage under its traditional form placed the woman under her husband's authority, or *manus*. He could divorce her on grounds of adultery, drinking wine, or stealing from the household, but she could not divorce him. She could neither possess property in her own right nor bequeath any to her children upon her death. When her husband died, the household property passed not to her but to his male heirs. And when her father died, she had no claim to any family inheritance, which was directed to her brothers or more remote male relatives. The effect of these laws was to exclude women from civil society, itself based on property ownership.

In the later republican and imperial periods, these rules were significantly modified. Women rarely married according to the traditional form but according to the form of "free" marriage. That practice allowed a woman to remain under her father's authority, to possess property given her by her father (most frequently the "dowry," recoverable from the husband's household in the event of his death), and to inherit from her father. She could also bequeath property to her own children and divorce her husband, just as he could divorce her.

Despite this greater freedom, women still suffered enormous disability under Roman law. Heirs could belong only to the father's side, never the mother's. Moreover, although she could bequeath her property to her children, she could not establish a line of succession in doing so. A woman was "the beginning and end of her own family," said the jurist Ulpian. Moreover, women could play no public role. They could not hold public office, represent anyone in a legal case, or even witness a will. Women had only a private existence and no public personality.

The dowry system, the guardian, women's limited ability to transmit wealth, and total political disability are all features of Roman law adopted, although modified according to local customary laws, by the medieval communities of western Europe.

CHRISTIAN DOCTRINE AND WOMEN'S PLACE. The Hebrew Bible and the Christian New Testament authorized later writers to limit women to the realm of the family and to burden them with the guilt of original sin. The passages most fruitful for this purpose were the creation narratives in Genesis and sentences from the Epistles defining women's role within the Christian family and community.

Each of the first two chapters of Genesis contains a creation narrative. In the first, "God created man in his own image, in the image of God he created him; male and female he created them" (New Revised Standard Version,

Gen. 1:27). In the second, God created Eve from Adam's rib (2:21–23). Christian theologians relied principally on Genesis 2 for their understanding of the relation between man and woman, interpreting the creation of Eve from Adam as proof of her subordination to him.

The creation story in Genesis 2 leads to that of the temptations in Genesis 3: of Eve by the wily serpent and of Adam by Eve. As read by Christian theologians from Tertullian to Thomas Aquinas, the narrative made Eve responsible for the Fall and its consequences. She instigated the act; she deceived her husband; she suffered the greater punishment. Her disobedience made it necessary for Jesus to be incarnated and to die on the cross. From the pulpit, moralists and preachers for centuries conveyed to women the guilt that they bore for original sin.

The Epistles offered advice to early Christians on building communities of the faithful. Among the matters to be regulated was the place of women. Paul offered views favorable to women in Galatians 3:28: "There is neither Jew nor Greek, there is neither slave nor free, there is neither male nor female; for you are all one in Christ Jesus." Paul also referred to women as his coworkers and placed them on a par with himself and his male coworkers (Phil. 4:2–3; Rom. 16:1–3; I Cor. 16:19). Elsewhere, Paul limited women's possibilities: "But I want you to understand that the head of every man is Christ, the head of a woman is her husband, and the head of Christ is God" (I Cor. 11:3).

Biblical passages by later writers (though attributed to Paul) enjoined women to forgo jewels, expensive clothes, and elaborate coiffures; and they forbade women to "teach or have authority over men," telling them to "learn in silence with all submissiveness," as is proper for one responsible for sin, consoling them, however, with the thought that they will be saved through childbearing (I Tim. 2:9–15). Other texts among the later Epistles defined women as the weaker sex and emphasized their subordination to their husbands (I Pet. 3:7; Col. 3:18; Eph. 5:22–23).

These passages from the New Testament became the arsenal employed by theologians of the early church to transmit negative attitudes toward women to medieval Christian culture—above all, Tertullian ("On the Apparel of Women"), Jerome (*Against Jovinian*), and Augustine (*The Literal Meaning of Genesis*).

THE IMAGE OF WOMEN IN MEDIEVAL LITERATURE. The philosophical, legal, and religious traditions born in antiquity formed the basis of the medieval intellectual synthesis wrought by trained thinkers, mostly clerics,

writing in Latin and based largely in universities. The vernacular literary tradition that developed alongside the learned tradition also spoke about female nature and women's roles. Medieval stories, poems, and epics also portrayed women negatively—as lustful and deceitful—while praising good housekeepers and loyal wives as replicas of the Virgin Mary or the female saints and martyrs.

There is an exception in the movement of "courtly love" that evolved in southern France from the twelfth century. Courtly love was the erotic love between a nobleman and noblewoman, the latter usually superior in social rank. It was always adulterous. From the conventions of courtly love derive modern Western notions of romantic love. The phenomenon has had an impact disproportionate to its size, for it affected only a tiny elite, and very few women. The exaltation of the female lover probably does not reflect a higher evaluation of women or a step toward their sexual liberation. More likely it gives expression to the social and sexual tensions besetting the knightly class at a specific historic juncture.

The literary fashion of courtly love was on the wane by the thirteenth century, when the widely read *Romance of the Rose* was composed in French by two authors of significantly different dispositions. Guillaume de Lorris composed the initial four thousand verses around 1235, and Jean de Meun added about seventeen thousand verses—more than four times the original —around 1265.

The fragment composed by Guillaume de Lorris stands squarely in the courtly love tradition. Here the poet, in a dream, is admitted into a walled garden where he finds a magic fountain in which a rosebush is reflected. He longs to pick one rose, but the thorns around it prevent his doing so, even as he is wounded by arrows from the God of Love, whose commands he agrees to obey. The remainder of this part of the poem recounts the poet's unsuccessful efforts to pluck the rose.

The longer part of the *Romance* by Jean de Meun also describes a dream. But here allegorical characters give long didactic speeches, providing a social satire on a variety of themes, including those pertaining to women. Love is an anxious and tormented state, the poem explains, women are greedy and manipulative, marriage is miserable, beautiful women are lustful, ugly ones cease to please, and a chaste woman, as rare as a black swan, can scarcely be found.

Shortly after Jean de Meun completed *The Romance of the Rose*, Mathéolus penned his *Lamentations*, a long Latin diatribe against marriage translated into French about a century later. The *Lamentations* sum up medieval attitudes

toward women and provoked the important response by Christine de Pizan in her *Book of the City of Ladies*.

In 1355 Giovanni Boccaccio wrote *Il Corbaccio*, another antifeminist manifesto, though ironically by an author whose other works pioneered new directions in Renaissance thought. The former husband of his lover appears to Boccaccio, condemning his unmoderated lust and detailing the defects of women. Boccaccio concedes at the end "how much men naturally surpass women in nobility" and is cured of his desires.[3]

WOMEN'S ROLES: THE FAMILY. The negative perceptions of women expressed in the intellectual tradition are also implicit in the actual roles that women played in European society. Assigned to subordinate positions in the household and the church, they were barred from significant participation in public life.

Medieval European households, like those in antiquity and in non-Western civilizations, were headed by males. It was the male serf (or peasant), feudal lord, town merchant, or citizen who was polled or taxed or succeeded to an inheritance or had any acknowledged public role, although their wives or widows could stand on a temporary basis as surrogates for them. From about 1100, the position of property-holding males was enhanced further: inheritance was confined to the male, or agnate, line—with depressing consequences for women.

A wife never fully belonged to her husband's family, nor was she a daughter to her father's family. She left her father's house young to marry whomever her parents chose. Her dowry was managed by her husband and normally passed to her children by him at her death.

A married woman's life was occupied nearly constantly with cycles of pregnancy, childbearing, and lactation. Women bore children through all the years of their fertility, and many died in childbirth before the end of that term. They also bore responsibility for raising young children up to six or seven. That responsibility was shared in the propertied classes, since it was common for a wet nurse to take over the job of breast-feeding, and servants took over other chores.

Women trained their daughters in the household responsibilities appropriate to their status, nearly always in tasks associated with textiles: spinning, weaving, sewing, embroidering. Their sons were sent out of the house as apprentices or students, or their training was assumed by fathers in later

---

3. Giovanni Boccaccio, *The Corbaccio; or, The Labyrinth of Love*, trans. and ed. Anthony K. Cassell, rev. ed. (Binghamton, N.Y., 1993), 71.

childhood and adolescence. On the death of her husband, a woman's children became the responsibility of his family. She generally did not take "his" children with her to a new marriage or back to her father's house, except sometimes in artisan classes.

Women also worked. Rural peasants performed farm chores, merchant wives often practiced their husband's trade, the unmarried daughters of the urban poor worked as servants or prostitutes. All wives produced or embellished textiles and did the housekeeping, while wealthy ones managed servants. These labors were unpaid or poorly paid but often contributed substantially to family wealth.

WOMEN'S ROLES: THE CHURCH. Membership in a household, whether a father's or a husband's, meant for women a lifelong subordination to others. In western Europe, the Roman Catholic Church offered an alternative to the career of wife and mother. A woman could enter a convent, parallel in function to the monasteries for men that evolved in the early Christian centuries.

In the convent, a woman pledged herself to a celibate life, lived according to strict community rules, and worshiped daily. Often the convent offered training in Latin, allowing some women to become considerable scholars and authors, as well as scribes, artists, and musicians. For women who chose the conventual life, the benefits could be enormous, but for numerous others placed in convents by paternal choice, the life could be restrictive and burdensome.

The conventual life declined as an alternative for women as the modern age approached. Reformed monastic institutions resisted responsibility for related female orders. The church increasingly restricted female institutional life by insisting on closer male supervision.

Women often sought other options. Some joined the communities of laywomen that sprang up spontaneously in the thirteenth century in the urban zones of western Europe, especially in Flanders and Italy. Some joined the heretical movements that flourished in late medieval Christendom, whose anticlerical and often antifamily positions particularly appealed to women. In these communities, some women were acclaimed as "holy women" or "saints," while others often were condemned as frauds or heretics.

In all, though the options offered to women by the church were sometimes less than satisfactory, sometimes they were richly rewarding. After 1520 the convent remained an option only in Roman Catholic territories. Protestantism engendered an ideal of marriage as a heroic endeavor and appeared to place husband and wife on a more equal footing. Sermons and treatises, however, still called for female subordination and obedience.

THE OTHER VOICE, 1300–1700

When the modern era opened, European culture was so firmly structured by a framework of negative attitudes toward women that to dismantle it was a monumental labor. The process began as part of a larger cultural movement that entailed the critical reexamination of ideas inherited from the ancient and medieval past. The humanists launched that critical reexamination.

THE HUMANIST FOUNDATION. Originating in Italy in the fourteenth century, humanism quickly became the dominant intellectual movement in Europe. Spreading in the sixteenth century from Italy to the rest of Europe, it fueled the literary, scientific, and philosophical movements of the era and laid the basis for the eighteenth-century Enlightenment.

Humanists regarded the scholastic philosophy of medieval universities as out of touch with the realities of urban life. They found in the rhetorical discourse of classical Rome a language adapted to civic life and public speech. They learned to read, speak, and write classical Latin and, eventually, classical Greek. They founded schools to teach others to do so, establishing the pattern for elementary and secondary education for the next three hundred years.

In the service of complex government bureaucracies, humanists employed their skills to write eloquent letters, deliver public orations, and formulate public policy. They developed new scripts for copying manuscripts and used the new printing press for the dissemination of texts, for which they created methods of critical editing.

Humanism was a movement led by males who accepted the evaluation of women in ancient texts and generally shared the misogynist perceptions of their culture. (Female humanists, as will be seen, did not.) Yet humanism also opened the door to a reevaluation of the nature and capacity of women. By calling authors, texts, and ideas into question, it made possible the fundamental rereading of the whole intellectual tradition that was required in order to free women from cultural prejudice and social subordination.

A DIFFERENT CITY. The other voice first appeared when, after so many centuries, the accumulation of misogynist concepts evoked a response from a capable woman female defender: Christine de Pizan (1365–1431). Introducing her *Book of the City of Ladies* (1405), she described how she was affected by reading Mathéolus's *Lamentations*: "Just the sight of this book . . . made me wonder how it happened that so many different men . . . are so inclined to express both in speaking and in their treatises and writings so many wicked

insults about women and their behavior. . . ." These statements impelled her to detest herself "and the entire feminine sex, as though we were monstrosities in nature."[4]

The remainder of the *Book of the City of Ladies* presents a justification of the female sex and a vision of an ideal community of women. A pioneer, she has not simply received the message of female inferiority but, rather, she rejects it. From the fourteenth to the seventeenth century, a huge body of literature accumulated that responded to the dominant tradition.

The result was a literary explosion consisting of works by both men and women, in Latin and in the vernaculars: works enumerating the achievements of notable women; works rebutting the main accusations made against women; works arguing for the equal education of men and women; works defining and redefining women's proper role in the family, at court, in public, describing women's lives and experiences. Recent monographs and articles have begun to hint at the great range of this phenomenon, involving probably several thousand titles. The protofeminism of these "other voices" constitutes a significant fraction of the literary product of the early modern era.

THE CATALOGS. Around 1365 the same Boccaccio whose *Corbaccio* rehearses the usual charges against female nature wrote another work, *Concerning Famous Women*. A humanist treatise drawing on classical texts, it praised 106 notable women, ninety-eight of them from pagan Greek and Roman antiquity, one (Eve) from the Bible, and seven from the medieval religious and cultural tradition; his book helped make all readers aware of a sex normally condemned or forgotten. Boccaccio's outlook, nevertheless, is unfriendly to women, for it singled out for praise those women who possessed the traditional virtues of chastity, silence, and obedience. Women who were active in the public realm, for example, rulers and warriors, were depicted as usually lascivious and as suffering terrible punishments for entering into the masculine sphere. Women were his subject, but Boccaccio's standard remained male.

Christine de Pizan's *Book of the City of Ladies* contains a second catalog, one responding specifically to Boccaccio's. Where Boccaccio portrays female virtue as exceptional, she depicts it as universal. Many women in history were leaders, or remained chaste despite the lascivious approaches of men, or were visionaries and brave martyrs.

The work of Boccaccio inspired a series of catalogs of illustrious women of the biblical, classical, Christian, and local past, among them Filippo da

---

4. Christine de Pizan, *The Book of the City of Ladies*, trans. Earl Jeffrey Richards, foreword by Marina Warner (New York, 1982), 1.1.1 (pp. 3–4), 1.1.1–2 (p. 5).

Bergamo's *Of Illustrious Women*, Pierre de Brantôme's *Lives of Illustrious Women*, Pierre Le Moyne's *Gallerie of Heroic Women*, and Pietro Paolo de Ribera's *Immortal Triumphs and Heroic Enterprises of 845 Women*. Whatever their embedded prejudices, these catalogs of illustrious women drove home to the public the possibility of female excellence.

THE DEBATE. At the same time, many questions remained: Could a woman be virtuous? Could she perform noteworthy deeds? Was she even, strictly speaking, of the same human species as men? These questions were debated over four centuries, in French, German, Italian, Spanish, and English, by authors male and female, among Catholics, Protestants, and Jews, in ponderous volumes and breezy pamphlets. The whole literary phenomenon has been called the *querelle des femmes*, the "woman question."

The opening volley of this battle occurred in the first years of the fifteenth century, in a literary debate sparked by Christine de Pizan. She exchanged letters critical of Jean de Meun's contribution to the *Romance of the Rose* with two French royal secretaries, Jean de Montreuil and Gontier Col. When the matter became public, Jean Gerson, one of Europe's leading theologians, supported de Pizan's arguments against de Meun, for the moment silencing the opposition.

The debate resurfaced repeatedly over the next two hundred years. *The Triumph of Women* (1438) by Juan Rodríguez de la Camara (or Juan Rodríguez del Padron) struck a new note by presenting arguments for the superiority of women to men. *The Champion of Women* (1440–42) by Martin Le Franc addresses once again the negative views of women presented in *The Romance of the Rose* and offers counterevidence of female virtue and achievement.

A cameo of the debate on women is included in the *Courtier*, one of the most read books of the era, published by the Italian Baldassare Castiglione in 1528 and immediately translated into other European vernaculars. The *Courtier* depicts a series of evenings at the court of the duke of Urbino in which many men and some women of the highest social stratum amuse themselves by discussing a range of literary and social issues. The "woman question" is a pervasive theme throughout, and the third of its four books is devoted entirely to that issue.

In a verbal duel, Gasparo Pallavicino and Giuliano de' Medici present the main claims of the two traditions. Gasparo argues the innate inferiority of women and their inclination to vice. Only in bearing children do they profit the world. Giuliano counters that women share the same spiritual and mental capacities as men and may excel in wisdom and action. Men and women are of the same essence: just as no stone can be more perfectly a stone than another, so no human being can be more perfectly human than

others, whether male or female. It was an astonishing assertion, boldly made to an audience as large as all Europe.

THE TREATISES. Humanism provided the materials for a positive counterconcept to the misogyny embedded in scholastic philosophy and law and inherited from the Greek, Roman, and Christian pasts. A series of humanist treatises on marriage and family, on education and deportment, and on the nature of women helped construct these new perspectives.

The works by Francesco Barbaro and Leon Battista Alberti—*On Marriage* (1415) and *On the Family* (1434–37), respectively—far from defending female equality, reasserted women's responsibilities for rearing children and managing the housekeeping while being obedient, chaste, and silent. Nevertheless, they served the cause of reexamining the issue of women's nature by placing domestic issues at the center of scholarly concern and reopening the pertinent classical texts. In addition, Barbaro emphasized the companionate nature of marriage and the importance of a wife's spiritual and mental qualities for the well-being of the family.

These themes reappear in later humanist works on marriage and the education of women by Juan Luis Vives and Erasmus. Both were moderately sympathetic to the condition of women, without reaching beyond the usual masculine prescriptions for female behavior.

An outlook more favorable to women characterizes the nearly unknown work *In Praise of Women* (ca. 1487) by the Italian humanist Bartolommeo Goggio. In addition to providing a catalog of illustrious women, Goggio argued that male and female are the same in essence, but that women (reworking from quite a new angle the Adam and Eve narrative) are actually superior. In the same vein, the Italian humanist Maria Equicola asserted the spiritual equality of men and women in *On Women* (1501). In 1525 Galeazzo Flavio Capra (or Capella) published his work *On the Excellence and Dignity of Women.* This humanist tradition of treatises defending the worthiness of women culminates in the work of Henricus Cornelius Agrippa *On the Nobility and Preeminence of the Female Sex.* No work by a male humanist more succinctly or explicitly presents the case for female dignity.

THE WITCH BOOKS. While humanists grappled with the issues pertaining to women and family, other learned men turned their attention to what they perceived as a very great problem: witches. Witch-hunting manuals, explorations of the witch phenomenon, and even defenses of witches are not at first glance pertinent to the tradition of the other voice. But they do relate in this way: most accused witches were women. The hostility aroused by supposed witch activity is comparable to the hostility aroused by women.

The evil deeds the victims of the hunt were charged with were exaggerations of the vices to which, many believed, all women were prone.

The connection between the witch accusation and the hatred of women is explicit in the notorious witch-hunting manual *The Hammer of Witches* (1486) by two Dominican inquisitors, Heinrich Krämer and Jacob Sprenger. Here the inconstancy, deceitfulness, and lustfulness traditionally associated with women are depicted in exaggerated form as the core features of witch behavior. These traits inclined women to make a bargain with the devil—sealed by sexual intercourse—by which they acquired unholy powers. Such bizarre claims, far from being rejected by rational men, were broadcast by intellectuals. The German Ulrich Molitur, the Frenchman Nicolas Rémy, and the Italian Stefano Guazzo all coolly informed the public of sinister orgies and midnight pacts with the devil. The celebrated French jurist, historian, and political philosopher Jean Bodin argued that because women were especially prone to diabolism, regular legal procedures could properly be suspended in order to try those accused of this "exceptional crime."

A few experts raised their voices in protest, such as the physician Johann Weyer, a student of Agrippa's. In 1563 he explained the witch phenomenon thus, without discarding belief in diabolism: the devil deluded foolish old women afflicted by melancholia, causing them to believe that they had magical powers. Weyer's rational skepticism, which had good credibility in the community of the learned, worked to revise the conventional views of women and witchcraft.

WOMEN'S WORKS. To the many categories of works produced on the question of women's worth must be added nearly all works written by women. A woman writing was in herself a statement of women's claim to dignity.

Only a few women wrote anything prior to the dawn of the modern era, for three reasons. First, they rarely received the education that would enable them to write. Second, they were not admitted to the public roles—as administrator, bureaucrat, lawyer or notary, or university professor—in which they might gain knowledge of the kinds of things the literate public thought worth writing about. Third, the culture imposed silence upon women and considered speaking out a form of unchastity. Given these conditions, it is remarkable that any women wrote. Those who did before the fourteenth century were almost always nuns or religious women whose isolation made their pronouncements more acceptable.

From the fourteenth century on, the volume of women's writings crescendoed. Women continued to write devotional literature, although not always as cloistered nuns. They also wrote diaries, often intended as keep-

sakes for their children; books of advice to their sons and daughters; letters to family members and friends; and family memoirs, in a few cases elaborate enough to be considered histories.

A few women wrote works directly concerning the "woman question," and some of these, such as the humanists Isotta Nogarola, Cassandra Fedele, Laura Cereta, and Olympia Morata, were highly trained. A few were professional writers, living by the income of their pen—the very first among them being Christine de Pizan, noteworthy in this context as in so many others. In addition to *The Book of the City of Ladies* and her critiques of *The Romance of the Rose,* she wrote *The Treasure of the City of Ladies* (a guide to social decorum for women), an advice book for her son, much courtly verse, and a full-scale history of the reign of King Charles V of France.

WOMEN PATRONS. Women who did not themselves write, but encouraged others to do so, boosted the development of an alternative tradition. Highly placed women patrons supported authors, artists, musicians, poets, and learned men. Such patrons, drawn mostly from the Italian elites and the courts of northern Europe, figure disproportionately as the dedicatees of the important works of early feminism.

For a start, it might be noted that the catalogs of Boccaccio and Alvaro de Luna were dedicated to the Florentine noblewoman Andrea Acciaiuoli and Doña María, first wife of King Juan II of Castile, while the French translation of Boccaccio's work was commissioned by Anne of Brittany, wife of King Charles VIII of France. The humanist treatises of Goggio, Equicola, Vives, and Agrippa were dedicated, respectively, to Eleanora of Aragon, wife of Ercole I d'Este, duke of Ferrara; to Margherita Cantelma of Mantua; to Catherine of Aragon, wife of King Henry VIII of England; and to Margaret, duchess of Austria and regent of the Netherlands. As late as 1696, Mary Astell's *Serious Proposal to the Ladies, for the Advancement of Their True and Greatest Interest* was dedicated to Princess Ann of Denmark.

These authors presumed that their efforts would be welcome to female patrons, or they may have written at the bidding of those patrons. Silent themselves, perhaps even unresponsive, these loftily placed women helped shape the tradition of the other voice.

THE ISSUES. The literary forms and patterns in which the tradition of the other voice presented itself have now been sketched. It remains to highlight the major issues around which this tradition crystallizes. In brief, there are four problems to which our authors return again and again, in plays and catalogs, in verse and in letters, in treatises and dialogues, in every language:

the problem of chastity; the problem of power; the problem of speech; and the problem of knowledge. Of these the greatest, preconditioning the others, is the problem of chastity.

THE PROBLEM OF CHASTITY. In traditional European culture, as in those of antiquity and others around the globe, chastity was perceived as woman's quintessential virtue—in contrast to courage, or generosity, or leadership, or rationality, seen as virtues characteristic of men. Opponents of women charged them with insatiable lust. Women themselves and their defenders—without disputing the validity of the standard—responded that women were capable of chastity.

The requirement of chastity kept women at home, silenced them, isolated them, left them in ignorance. It was the source of all other impediments. Why was it so important to the society of men, of whom chastity was not required, and who, more often than not, considered it their right to violate the chastity of any woman they encountered?

Female chastity ensured the continuity of the male-headed household. If a man's wife was not chaste, he could not be sure of the legitimacy of his offspring. If they were not his and they acquired his property, it was not his household, but some other man's, that had endured. If his daughter was not chaste, she could not be transferred to another man's household as his wife, and he was dishonored.

The whole system of the integrity of the household and the transmission of property was bound up in female chastity. Such a requirement only had an impact on property-owning classes, of course. Poor women could not expect to maintain their chastity, least of all if they were in contact with high-status men to whom all women but those of their own household were prey.

In Catholic Europe, the requirement of chastity was further buttressed by moral and religious imperatives. Original sin was inextricably linked with the sexual act. Virginity was seen as heroic virtue, far more impressive than, say, the avoidance of idleness or greed. Monasticism, the cultural institution that dominated medieval Europe for centuries, was grounded in the renunciation of the flesh. The Catholic reform of the eleventh century imposed a similar standard on all the clergy and a heightened awareness of sexual requirements on all the laity. Although men were asked to be chaste, female unchastity was much worse: it led to the devil, as Eve had led mankind to sin.

To such requirements, women and their defenders protested their innocence. Furthermore, following the example of holy women who had escaped the requirements of family and sought the religious life, some women began to conceive of female communities as alternatives both to family and to the cloister. Christine de Pizan's city of ladies was such a community. Moderata Fonte and Mary Astell envisioned others. The luxurious salons of the French

précieuses of the seventeenth century, or the comfortable English drawing rooms of the next, may have been born of the same impulse. Here women might not only escape, if briefly, the subordinate position that life in the family entailed, but they might make claims to power, exercise their capacity for speech, and display their knowledge.

THE PROBLEM OF POWER. Women were excluded from power: the whole cultural tradition insisted on it. Only men were citizens, only men bore arms, only men could be chiefs or lords or kings. There were exceptions, which did not disprove the rule, when wives or widows or mothers took the place of men, awaiting their return or the maturation of a male heir. A woman who attempted to rule in her own right was perceived as an anomaly, a monster, at once a deformed woman and an insufficient male, sexually confused and, consequently, unsafe.

The association of such images with women who held or sought power explains some otherwise odd features of early modern culture. Queen Elizabeth I of England, one of the few women to hold full regal authority in European history, played with such male/female images — positive ones, of course — in representing herself to her subjects. She was a prince, and manly, even though she was female. She was also (she claimed) virginal, a condition absolutely essential if she was to avoid the attacks of her opponents. Catherine de' Medici, who ruled France as widow and regent for her sons, also adopted such imagery in defining her position. She chose as one symbol the figure of Artemisia, an androgynous ancient warrior-heroine, who combined a female persona with masculine powers.

Power in a woman, without such sexual imagery, seems to have been indigestible by the culture. A rare note was struck by the Englishman Sir Thomas Elyot in his *Defence of Good Women* (1540), justifying both women's participation in civic life and prowess in arms. The old tune was sung by the Scots reformer John Knox in his *First Blast of the Trumpet against the Monstrous Regiment of Women* (1558), for whom rule by women, defects in nature, was a hideous contradiction in terms.

The confused sexuality of the imagery of female potency was not reserved for rulers. Any woman who excelled was likely to be called an Amazon, recalling the self-mutilated warrior women of antiquity who repudiated all men, gave up their sons, and raised only their daughters. She was often said to have "exceeded her sex" or to have possessed "masculine virtue" — as the very fact of conspicuous excellence conferred masculinity, even on the female subject. The catalogs of notable women often showed those female heroes dressed in armor, armed to the teeth, like men. Amazonian heroines romp through the epics of the age — Ariosto's *Orlando Furioso* (1532) and Spenser's *Faerie Queene* (1590–1609). Excellence in a woman was perceived

as a claim for power, and power was reserved for the masculine realm. A woman who possessed either was masculinized and lost title to her own female identity.

THE PROBLEM OF SPEECH. Just as power had a sexual dimension when it was claimed by women, so did speech. A good woman spoke little. Excessive speech was an indication of unchastity. By speech, women seduced men. Eve had lured Adam into sin by her speech. Accused witches were commonly accused of having spoken abusively, or irrationally, or simply too much. As enlightened a figure as Francesco Barbaro insisted on silence in a woman, which he linked to her perfect unanimity with her husband's will and her unblemished virtue (i.e., her chastity). Another Italian humanist, Leonardo Bruni, in advising a noblewoman on her studies, barred her not from speech but from public speaking. That was reserved for men.

Related to the problem of speech was that of costume—another, if silent, form of self-expression. Assigned the task of pleasing men as their primary occupation, elite women often tended toward elaborate costume, hairdressing, and the use of cosmetics. Clergy and secular moralists alike condemned these practices. The appropriate function of costume and adornment was to announce the status of a woman's husband or father. Any further indulgence in adornment was akin to unchastity.

THE PROBLEM OF KNOWLEDGE. When the Italian noblewoman Isotta Nogarola had begun to attain a reputation as a humanist, she was accused of incest—a telling instance of the association of learning in women with unchastity. That chilling association inclined any woman who was educated to deny that she was or to make exaggerated claims of heroic chastity.

If educated women were pursued with suspicions of sexual misconduct, women seeking an education faced an even more daunting obstacle: the assumption that women were by nature incapable of learning, that reason was a particularly masculine ability. Just as they proclaimed their chastity, women and their defenders insisted on their capacity for learning. The major work by a male writer on female education—that by Juan Luis Vives, *On the Education of a Christian Woman* (1523)—granted female capacity for intellection but still argued that a woman's whole education was to be shaped around the requirement of chastity and a future within the household. Female writers of the next generations—Marie de Gournay in France, Anna Maria van Schurman in Holland, Mary Astell in England—began to envision other possibilities.

The pioneers of female education were the Italian women humanists who managed to attain a Latin literacy and knowledge of classic and Christian literature equivalent to that of prominent men. Their works implicitly and explicitly raise questions about women's social roles, defining problems that

beset women attempting to break out of the cultural limits that had bound them. Like Christine de Pizan, who achieved an advanced education through her father's tutoring and her own devices, their bold questioning makes clear the importance of training. Only when women were educated to the same standard as male leaders would they be able to raise that other voice and insist on their dignity as human beings morally, intellectually, and legally equal to men.

THE OTHER VOICE. The other voice, a voice of protest, was mostly female, but it was also male. It spoke in the vernaculars and in Latin, in treatises and dialogues, in plays and poetry, in letters and diaries, and in pamphlets. It battered at the wall of prejudice that encircled women and raised a banner announcing its claims. The female was equal to (or even superior to) the male in essential nature—moral, spiritual, intellectual. Women were capable of higher education, of holding positions of power and influence in the public realm, and of speaking and writing persuasively. The last bastion of masculine supremacy, centered on the notions of a woman's primary domestic responsibility and the requirement of female chastity, was not as yet assaulted—although visions of productive female communities as alternatives to the family indicated an awareness of the problem.

During the period 1300–1700, the other voice remained only a voice, and one only dimly heard. It did not result—yet—in an alteration of social patterns. Indeed, to this day, they have not entirely been altered. Yet the call for justice issued as long as six centuries ago by those writing in the tradition of the other voice must be recognized as the source and origin of the mature feminist tradition and of the realignment of social institutions accomplished in the modern age.

We would like to thank the volume editors in this series, who responded with many suggestions to an earlier draft of this introduction, making it a collaborative enterprise. Many of their suggestions and criticisms have resulted in revisions of this introduction, though we remain responsible for the final product.

PROJECTED TITLES IN THE SERIES

Giuseppa Eleonora Barbapiccola and Diamante Medaglia Faini, *The Education of Women*, edited and translated by Rebecca Messbarger

Francesco Barbaro et al., *On Marriage and the Family*, edited and translated by Margaret L. King

Laura Battiferra, *Selected Poetry, Prose, and Letters*, edited and translated by Victoria Kirkham

Giulia Bigolina, *Urania*, edited and translated by Valeria Finucci

Elisabetta Caminer Turra, *Writings on and about Women*, edited and translated by Catherine Sama

Maddalena Campiglia, *Flori*, edited and translated by Virginia Cox with Lisa Sampson

Rosalba Carriera, *Letters, Diaries, and Art*, edited and translated by Shearer West

Madame du Chatelet, *Selected Works*, edited by Judith Zinsser

Christine de Pizan et al., *Debate over the "Romance of the Rose,"* edited and translated by Tom Conley with Elisabeth Hodges

Christine de Pizan, *Life of Charles V*, edited and translated by Charity Cannon Willard

Christine de Pizan, *The Long Road of Learning*, edited and translated by Andrea Tarnowski

Gabrielle de Coignard, *Spiritual Sonnets*, edited and translated by Melanie E. Gregg

Vittoria Colonna, *Sonnets for Michelangelo*, edited and translated by Abigail Brundin

Vittoria Colonna, Chiara Matraini, and Lucrezia Marinella, *Marian Writings*, edited and translated by Susan Haskins

Marie Dentière, *Epistles*, edited and translated by Mary B. McKinley

Marie-Catherine Desjardins (Madame de Villedieu), *Memoirs of the Life of Henriette-Sylvie de Molière*, edited and translated by Donna Kuizenga

Princess Elizabeth of Bohemia, *Correspondence with Descartes*, edited and translated by Lisa Shapiro

Fairy-Tales by Seventeenth-Century French Women Writers, edited and translated by Lewis Seifert and Domna C. Stanton

Isabella d'Este, *Selected Letters*, edited and translated by Deanna Shemek

Moderata Fonte, *Floridoro*, edited and translated by Valeria Finucci and Julia Kisacky

Moderata Fonte and Lucrezia Marinella, *Religious Narratives*, edited and translated by Virginia Cox

Francisca de los Apostoles, *Visions on Trial: The Inquisitional Trial of Francisca de los Apostoles*, edited and translated by Gillian T. W. Ahlgren

Catharina Regina von Greiffenberg, *Meditations on the Life of Christ*, edited and translated by Lynne Tatlock

Annibale Guasco, *Discourse to Lady Lavinia His Daughter concerning the Manner in Which She Should Conduct Herself at Court*, edited and translated by Peggy Osborn

Louise Labé, *Complete Works*, edited and translated by Annie Finch and Deborah Baker

Madame de Maintenon, *Lectures and Dramatic Dialogues*, edited and translated by John Conley, S.J.

Lucrezia Marinella, *L'Enrico; or, Byzantium Conquered*, edited and translated by Maria Galli Stampino

Lucrezia Marinella, *Happy Arcadia*, edited and translated by Susan Haskins and Letizia Panizza

Chiara Matraini, *Selected Poetry and Prose*, edited and translated by Elaine MacLachlan

Olympia Morata, *Complete Writings*, edited and translated by Holt N. Parker

Isotta Nogarola, *Selected Letters*, edited and translated by Margaret L. King and Diana Robin

Jacqueline Pascal, *"A Rule for Children" and Other Writings*, edited and translated by John Conley, S.J.

Eleonora Petersen von Merlau, *Autobiography* (1718), edited and translated by Barbara Becker-Cantarino

Alessandro Piccolomini, *Rethinking Marriage in Sixteenth-Century Italy*, edited and translated by Letizia Panizza

In Praise of Women: Italian Fifteenth-Century Defenses of Women, edited and translated by Daniel Bornstein

Madeleine and Catherine des Roches, *Selected Letters, Dialogues, and Poems*, edited and translated by Anne Larsen

Oliva Sabuco, *The New Philosophy: True Medicine*, edited and translated by Gianna Pomata

Margherita Sarrocchi, *La Scanderbeide*, edited and translated by Rinaldina Russell

Madeleine de Scudéry, *Orations and Rhetorical Dialogues*, edited and translated by Jane Donawerth with Julie Strongson

Madeleine de Scudéry, *Sapho*, edited and translated by Karen Newman

Justine Siegemund, *The Court Midwife of the Electorate of Brandenburg* (1690), edited and translated by Lynne Tatlock

Gabrielle Suchon, *"On Philosophy" and "On Morality,"* edited and translated by Domna Stanton with Rebecca Wilkin

Sara Copio Sullam, *Sara Copio Sullam: Jewish Poet and Intellectual in Early Seventeenth-Century Venice*, edited and translated by Don Harrán

Arcangela Tarabotti, *Convent Life as Inferno: A Report*, introduction and notes by Francesca Medioli, translated by Letizia Panizza

Francesco Buoninsegni and Arcangela Tarabotti, *Menippean Satire: "Against Feminine Extravagance" and "Antisatire,"* edited and translated by Elissa Weaver

Arcangela Tarabotti, *Paternal Tyranny*, edited and translated by Letizia Panizza

Laura Terracina, *Works*, edited and translated by Michael Sherberg

Katharina Schütz Zell, *Selected Writings*, edited and translated by Elsie McKee

ACKNOWLEDGMENTS

Roger Chartier, Christian Jouhaud, and François Lecercle offered advice on the transcription and punctuation of the French text. David Hult, Nancy K. Miller, and Peter Stallybrass suggested modifications to the translation. The winning translation of a particularly tricky phrase came to Annie Jones in a dream, and she was kind enough to share it with me. Lance Donaldson-Evans read the translation with such care and proposed so many essential modifications that he deserves far more than a mere acknowledgment. Thanks to Marilyn Rackley for her help on the first draft of the translation. Havivah Schwartz typed the manuscript onto disk.

I thank all of them for their help.

AGAINST MARRIAGE

INTRODUCTION
LA GRANDE MADEMOISELLE

In this world, although one can distinguish what is permanent from what is only a passing breeze, one should nonetheless heed the breeze, for sometimes it is more prudent to do so than to neglect it.

—Anne-Marie-Louise d'Orléans, duchesse de Montpensier, *Mémoires*

THE OTHER VOICE

In seventeenth-century France, these three rules were ironclad:

1. The life of any individual important enough to be received by the king was centered around court activities.

2. A woman who had the family connections and the financial assets necessary to enable her parents to negotiate a marriage on her behalf was obliged to accept their proposition—no matter how unappealing she found the man who had been selected for her.

3. Once married, the woman's life became, in legal terms, completely subservient to that of her husband. If she had any intellectual or artistic aspirations, she forgot them: a truly remarkable number of women writers were publishing in seventeenth-century France; not one of them managed to do so while maintaining a traditional marriage.

To break even one of these unwritten rules of conduct was already bold. To break all of them was quite simply unthinkable. And yet that was exactly the plan of action advised by the correspondence published for the first time in its entirety in this volume.

In early modern Europe, the marriage of an aristocratic woman was always a thoroughly political matter: it was understood by all concerned that she was first and foremost a commodity. She belonged to her family, whose role it was to negotiate the exchange of her hand for whatever it needed most—money, social advancement, a military alliance. The higher her rank,

the higher the stakes of these negotiations. And when great wealth and extensive property were added to the equation, such a marriage became truly an affair of state.

In seventeenth-century France, at the moment when the Bourbon monarchy was moving ever closer to absolutism, Anne-Marie-Louise d'Orléans, duchesse de Montpensier, was without rival as a marital commodity. To begin with, her lineage was the most noble of any contemporary French princess: she was the granddaughter of Henri IV and the daughter of Gaston d'Orléans, the brother of Louis XIII. In addition, she was by far the richest woman in France, wealthier than almost any French prince, and indeed she was probably the wealthiest woman in all Europe.[1] It is impossible, therefore, to overestimate her value to the French state.

That value, however, was not negotiable in the usual way, for Montpensier was, to an extent otherwise unheard of in her day, a free agent in the marital system. Almost all of her inheritance had come to her directly from her mother, Marie de Bourbon, duchesse de Montpensier—sole heiress to several fortunes amassed by the Montpensier family in the sixteenth century—who died within days of the birth of her only child. Montpensier was therefore thoroughly her own mistress, able to decide completely independently what would become of her person and her estates. True, her younger first cousin, Louis XIV, proposed, as kings traditionally did for all royal princesses, marriages that would have exchanged her hand for alliances strategic to the French state. In her case alone, however, he was unable to force her to accept any of his propositions. Montpensier was mindful of family concerns—what she calls in this correspondence her "first duties" (see p. 61)—but she refused to let her fate be dictated by them.

It is to Montpensier's control over her inheritance that we owe the correspondence published here, the only extended reflection on what the alliance system meant for the women who were the principal pawns in its game. That control made it possible for her to take a more personal view of royal unions: to meditate on the institution of marriage, its disadvantages as well as its advantages for women, and, most importantly, to consider how women might spend their lives if they did the unthinkable and decided not to marry. The following correspondence is the result of that meditation. Very much an "other" voice, it is a unique example from the early modern period of a

---

1. Vincent Pitts reviews Montpensier's total income and its sources in *La Grande Mademoiselle at the Court of France, 1627–1693* (Baltimore: Johns Hopkins University Press, 2000), 263–68. He estimates that the complete value of her assets was about 11 million livres, whereas the average fortune of a royal prince of the day was only 3 million livres. Only the Condé princes had greater wealth (266).

wealthy, independent woman's dreams of how she might improve her existence and that of other women if she were to refuse to allow herself to be exchanged as a marital commodity. It can be thought of as a feminist counter-
part to Thomas More's celebrated political essay *Utopia* (1516): Montpensier
imagines the ideal government as one under female control and the ideal
state as one perfectly responsive to women's concerns.

BIOGRAPHY

On the scene of seventeenth-century France, the woman referred to by her
contemporaries most often simply as Mademoiselle or La Grande Mademoiselle was truly a figure who was larger-than-life.[2] Beginning with her
birth at the Louvre, on May 29, 1627, her entire existence was played out as
public spectacle. Virtually from the start, the foremost question on her contemporaries' minds was the choice of her future husband. Debate on this issue was especially intense upon the birth of the future Louis XIV in 1638: his
mother, Anne of Austria, apparently suggested that the two cousins might
one day marry. Commentators usually dismiss this possibility as little more
than a joke. The fact remains, however, that it continued to be repeated, virtually until 1660 and the king's marriage, the event that initiated the correspondence edited here.

Beginning in 1644 when Montpensier was seventeen and Philip IV of
Spain became a widower, other candidates began to appear on the scene,

---

2. Montpensier owes the names by which her contemporaries referred to her to a curious practice that first began to function at the French court in her day and that was maintained until the
Revolution of 1789. In this naming system, the brother of the king was known simply as "Monsieur." (Montpensier's father, Gaston d'Orléans, was the first royal brother to be so known; contemporary references almost never mention his titles and speak only of "Monsieur.") Daughters
of the king were called "Madame" with their given name—"Madame Elisabeth," and so forth.
The royal niece, daughter of "Monsieur," became the first member of the court to be known
simply as "Mademoiselle"; the title stuck for the first eighteen years of her life, as long as she
was Monsieur's only daughter. Once he had other daughters by his second wife, she was referred to more often as "La Grande Mademoiselle." When they mention this second name, contemporary commentators all explain that it was a reference to her standing and was not intended as a reference to Montpensier's exceptional height—although everyone adds that she
was remarkably tall, in particular for a woman of her day. She apparently first became known
as "La Grande Mademoiselle" when the second man to be called "Monsieur," Louis XIV's brother
Philippe d'Anjou, wanted his oldest daughter to be known as "Mademoiselle." Rather than
follow seventeenth-century court custom, I refer to Anne-Marie-Louise d'Orléans, duchesse de
Montpensier, as "Montpensier." Male nobles of her day are now known by an abbreviated version of their titles: thus, François, duc de La Rochefoucauld, is today referred to as "La Rochefoucauld." There is no reason why we should maintain, as French literary history continues to
do, a separate onomastic code for his female contemporaries.

such as the Holy Roman Emperor, Ferdinand III, who was also widowed at about this time. No possible alliance was more seriously or more often proposed than that with Charles Stuart, future King Charles II of England, who joined his mother Henrietta Maria in her exile in France in 1646. All the proposed alliances failed to materialize for a variety of reasons: the emperor, for example, settled on another choice. Nevertheless, beginning with the possibility of a Stuart alliance, it becomes evident that the politics of marriage were shaping the young duchess's character. With Charles Stuart, we have the first example of a phenomenon recurrent during the next years of Montpensier's life: the match did not come off because she herself was against it. She quickly understood the attraction of her immense wealth for an impoverished exile dreaming of recapturing the English throne. She just as quickly concluded that the cost of that dream might prove prohibitive, that the carefully accumulated Montpensier assets could well be decimated in the process. In this way, the notion of personally taking control over her fate first became a reality for Montpensier.

Then, as of late 1648, another type of history came to dominate French political life so thoroughly that would-be alliances were suddenly sidelined. From the beginning, Montpensier was an eyewitness to the unfolding of the Fronde, the civil war that polarized French society until 1653. The Fronde was an unusually complicated uprising, during which various factions, all of which were allegedly united in their opposition—if not always specifically to the Crown, at least to royal authority in the person of the king's representative, Prime Minister Mazarin—sometimes reinforced but more often undermined one another's efforts. Certainly, the different factions never managed to work together in the way that would have been necessary for their cause to be successful. Any civil war profoundly destabilizes a society, making many things impossible, but at the same time making possible things that would never otherwise have taken place. Among the least expected consequences of the Fronde was surely the fact that during those tumultuous years, women from the highest ranks of the nobility participated in military actions to a degree unheard of in France before or since.

Among them, three duchesses—the duchesse de Chevreuse, the duchesse de Longueville, and the duchesse de Montpensier—were by far the most visible: all three rode at the head of armies and played key strategic roles. Their military daring was so striking that their contemporaries referred to them as Amazons, as though they were the legendary women warriors come to life. Thus, Montpensier managed to enter the city of Orléans by battering down the only gate no one had thought to fortify and thereby won that city over to the rebel cause. Later, in an exploit that quickly became

the stuff of legend, in July 1652 she gave the rebels, known as *frondeurs,* their final victory. The battle was raging throughout the streets of Paris between the vastly outnumbered opposition forces, led by their finest general, the prince de Condé, and the royal army, under the command of their leading general, Turenne. Louis XIV and Mazarin were watching from high ground just outside Paris, awaiting the seemingly inevitable massacre—when Montpensier issued orders to turn the cannon of the Bastille, which normally faced inward on the city, against the royal forces. Condé and the rebels were saved. And, as if to make certain that her first cousin the king would know who was responsible for his defeat, Montpensier—in this case, every inch the "grande" Mademoiselle—dominated the scene from the towers of the Bastille: she even added a large hat and long plumes to make her already notable stature more impressive still and guaranteed that she would be visible from a great distance.

We do not know exactly how the great *frondeuses* dressed when they led troops into battle. (When they were traveling incognito, fleeing the enemy, they often wore men's clothing.) Near the time of the Fronde and even much later in life, when Montpensier sat for portraits, she had herself represented in a quite dazzling mix of attire. Witness, for example, the portrait, clearly from her *frondeuse* period, by Charles and Henri Beaubrun (fig. 1). On the one hand, she cuts a stylish, even a glamorous figure, as if ready to take part in court festivities: she wears sweeping, diaphanous garments, an elaborately plumed hat, and magnificent, luminous pearls. On the other, she is also prepared for battle, since she carries both a shield and a lance and, artfully camouflaged by the swirls of lush fabric, she wears a breastplate (although it is hard to imagine how a breastplate so low-slung could have done much good!).[3]

As he stood at the king's side during Montpensier's ultimate rebellion, the episode at the Bastille, Mazarin is reported to have remarked that when she redirected the cannon, she "killed" her husband—that is, any chance that might have remained for that much-discussed marriage with Louis XIV. In fact, she had killed her chances for much more than that. By October Louis was once again firmly in control of his capital. Among his first initiatives upon regaining power, the king ordered all the rebel leaders into exile: thus it was that Montpensier found herself forcibly removed from the court, from public life, and from a chance at any alliance sponsored by the king. She would only be allowed to return to court in 1657, by which point—in a period in which aristocratic women generally married before they turned

3. A 1672 portrait, now at Versailles, by Pierre Bourguignon, still mixes court fashion and battle dress, although in a more traditional, allegorical vein (see fig. 2).

Fig. 1. Portrait of Anne-Marie-Louise d'Orléans, duchesse de Montpensier, known as La Grande Mademoiselle. Charles and Henri Beaubrun. Musée Carnavalet, Paris. Photo: Photothèque des Musées de la Ville de Paris/Habouzit.

twenty, and often much sooner—at age thirty, she had become a decidedly less attractive commodity.

Montpensier chose as the site of her exile one of her properties she had never before laid eyes on, the château at Saint-Fargeau. The years she spent in compulsory isolation from the place those of her rank considered the cen-

Fig. 2. Portrait of Anne-Marie-Louise d'Orléans, duchesse de Montpensier, holding the portrait of her father (1672). Pierre Bourguignon. Versailles, Musée national du Château et des Trianons. Photo: Réunion des Musées Nationaux/Art Resource, NY.

ter of the universe were hardly wasted: she developed new interests, architecture in particular, when she had the dilapidated château remodeled to her specifications. She surrounded herself with a true miniature court: she had the latest plays staged for her followers; she organized all the activities typical of contemporary court life—from dancing to hunting. Most important of all, by the time her exile had ended, she had discovered a literary talent,

one she might never have explored had she continued to live in the midst of all-consuming court intrigue. Montpensier even had a printing press set up in her château, and she was thus able to publish her early efforts herself.

Among those Montpensier frequented during her exile were two of the leading scholars of her century: Pierre-Daniel Huet and Jean Regnault de Segrais. By serving as intellectual mentors and collaborators to Madeleine de Scudéry and Marie-Madeleine Pioche de La Vergne, comtesse de Lafayette, the seventeenth century's most influential novelists, these two men—truly among the unsung heroes of the early modern tradition of French women's writing—played a decisive role in the development of prose fiction in France. Almost without exception—and Montpensier was most emphatically *not* one of those rare exceptions—women of her day had no formal education to speak of. Those women who became writers found either a male relative who oversaw their education or, when they were already adults, a scholar willing to help them make up for lost time. Without the collaboration of men such as Huet and Segrais, the most influential women writers of early modern France would never have been able to gain the familiarity with literary tradition that any author needs to acquire in order to produce his or her own fiction. In Montpensier's case, scholars encouraged her to read widely, to learn Italian (above all, in order to read Tasso in the original), and to begin to take her own writing seriously. Segrais in particular—who was a central member of Montpensier's court in exile—worked with her so closely during her authorial apprenticeship that today's specialists of French literature are still debating, on the one hand, the extent of Montpensier's participation in *Les Nouvelles françaises* (1657), an influential collection of short stories generally attributed to Segrais alone, and, on the other, of Segrais's collaboration on Montpensier's *Mémoires*.[4]

The question of who wrote exactly how much of each work is clearly unanswerable today. The fact remains that it was during her exile that Montpensier began the experiments with prose fiction that would continue to occupy her until the 1670s. More important still is the fact that it was at Saint-Fargeau that she began the composition of her major authorial achievement, the manuscript of the memoirs of her life on which she worked, off and on, virtually until her death in 1693.[5]

4. On the question of Montpensier's collaboration with Segrais, see my *Tender Geographies: Women and the Origins of the Novel in France* (New York: Columbia University Press, 1991), 52–55. For another view, see Jean Garapon, *La Grande Mademoiselle mémorialiste: Une Autobiographie dans le temps* (Geneva: Droz, 1989), 30–35.

5. Montpensier's memoirs were published only posthumously, initially in 1718, in an incomplete edition, next in 1728, in the first complete publication. This time lag is in no way sur-

By the end of her four years of political exile, Montpensier had become the woman we find in her correspondence with Françoise Bertaut de Motteville: someone who had thought a great deal about whether it was essential to live at her society's political and cultural nerve center, someone who had come to understand that it was important to her own sense of self not only to witness the unfolding of history, but also to bear witness to this process in writing. Thus, her memoirs—a canny blend of the narration of key events, the Fronde in particular, and personal reaction to those events—open with a detailed account of the process that had led her to shift her energies from the battlefield to the writing table:

> In the past, I had great difficulty imagining how anyone who was used to the court and born into the rank I was given at birth could occupy her mind, if she were reduced to living in the country: it had always seemed to me that nothing could take one's mind off things when one had been forced to leave [the court] and that, for great nobles, to find oneself outside the court meant to be completely alone. . . . However, since I have retired to my estate, I have been very happy to realize that . . . this time spent in seclusion is far from the least agreeable period of my life. . . . One finds there the leisure one needs to put things into writing. (C. 1:1–2, P. 40:367, B. 1:21)[6]

When Montpensier was finally allowed to return to court in the summer of 1657, she was thus a very different person from the politically rebellious princess who had gone into exile with such trepidation. She quickly gave

---

prising. It was only after Louis XIV's death in 1715 that memoirs dealing with his reign began to appear; the 1720s and 1730s witnessed the initial publication of almost all the memoirs that have come down to us. Since she writes extensively about the Fronde, the ultimate taboo subject for the Sun King, it was inconceivable that Montpensier's memoirs could have circulated in print before this time.

6. The various editions of Montpensier's memoirs follow different manuscripts and not always reliably. Adolphe Chéruel's 1858–59 edition (4 vols.; Paris: G. Charpentier) is by far the best, Claude Petitot's 1824–25 edition (4 vols.; Paris: Foucault) the next best. Christian Bouyer recently reissued Chéruel's text (2 vols.; Paris: Libraire Fontaine, 1985). Since none of these editions is widely available, when I cite Montpensier's *Mémoires,* I provide references to all three editions (labeled "C.," "P.," and "B."). I have slightly altered Montpensier's vocabulary in the passage just cited because the words she uses as synonyms for "exile"—"retirement," "retreat"—both have such different connotations today. In seventeenth-century French, these words—along with "repose" and "desert"—were used to mean political exile; they also signified, as is the case in the opening paragraph of Montpensier's memoirs, all the positive aspects of life away from the agitation of court life. On this vocabulary and its uses, see Domna Stanton, "The Ideal of 'repos' in Seventeenth-Century French Literature," *L'Esprit créateur* 15, nos. 1–2 (spring–summer 1975): 79–104.

official notification of that difference with her decision to leave the court again soon thereafter, this time of her own volition, for another of her estates, Champigny-sur-Veude. There, she turned her attention once again to literary pursuits: she began work on a project she later continued at Saint-Fargeau, a collective volume entitled *Divers portraits*, that she had privately published in January 1659.

Divers portraits gathers together fifty-nine verbal portraits and self-portraits, of which Montpensier herself contributed seventeen: these are biographical and autobiographical explorations of the most famous court figures of the day. It marked an important moment in the development of the modern novel: the emphasis on interiority and character development that characterizes these portraits soon became the trademark of the new French prose fiction. In addition, the volume can be seen as a collective statement, for it—along with two subsequent, more extensive collections, which had wider circulation—launched a number of literary careers. *Divers portraits* contains, for example, the first published work of the woman destined to compose *La Princesse de Clèves*, known as the first modern novel: Lafayette. Lafayette contributed to the collection the portrait of her lifelong best friend, Marie de Rabutin-Chantal, marquise de Sévigné, whose letters would become the most celebrated of the entire French tradition. A number of those published in these compilations were, like La Rochefoucauld, former leaders of the Fronde; others were, like Sévigné and Lafayette, members of *frondeur* families. When Montpensier launched the vogue for literary portraiture, it was as if she were indicating a redeployment of forces: those who had formerly actively participated in court politics would now pay written testimony to the psychology of their age.

While the portrait collections were still appearing, for the first time since her exile, Montpensier was called upon to take an active role in court life. During the early months of 1660, all the central members of the court were traveling, heading for a royal wedding. The twenty-two-year-old king was getting married to the Infanta of Spain, and their two countries, after having been at war for years, were to sign a peace treaty. A double ceremony was planned: the ceremony on Spanish soil on June 3, that in France on June 9. The court proceeded to the border with Spain in stately fashion, with extended stays along the way. Shortly after they reached their destination of Saint-Jean-de-Luz on May 8, against the backdrop of the ultimate marriage as political alliance, Montpensier records in her memoirs that she initiated first conversations and then a correspondence with Motteville on what she called "the project of a solitary way of life for individuals who would agree

to leave the court"—and agree never to marry (C. 3:453, P. 42:490, B. 2:146). Thus was born Montpensier's utopian vision for a community in which women would be mistresses of their fates and their property.

The first letter is dated May 14, two and a half weeks before the royal nuptials, but also less than two weeks shy of Montpensier's thirty-third birthday. Surely everyone present at Saint-Jean-de-Luz realized that her value as marital commodity was rapidly dwindling. Certainly, by this point Montpensier had come to think of marriage as an institution that was most often highly disadvantageous to women. The paragraph preceding her account of the correspondence's origin is devoted to the marriage of Princess Marguerite de Savoie with the duke of Parma: Montpensier describes the "little sovereign" as a "dishonest man" with only one "passion": "shoeing horses." She considered him unworthy of such a bride and suggests that the princess's destiny proves this point: "She did not survive this shame for long; she died shortly thereafter." Montpensier concludes that "she should never have married" (C. 3:452, P. 42:489, B. 2:146). During the protracted wedding festivities, the royal first cousin thus played a double role: in public, she was a key member of the French delegation, acting out every move of the complicated ceremonial role expected of her, at the same time as, in private, she was penning a violent protest against the institution of marriage as it functioned in her day.

In the aftermath of his marriage, Louis XIV set about firming up his control over his kingdom. He most definitely did not intend to lose the potential for negotiation represented by the vast Montpensier domain and thus proposed a final series of alliances to his ever-more recalcitrant cousin. Letter 5 of her correspondence with Motteville, written the year after the royal marriage, portrays Montpensier as caught between a woman's traditional obligation to her family and her newfound sense of obligation to herself; it also proves her continued conviction, initially expressed on the eve of the royal nuptials in her third letter, that marriage was a form of "slavery" for women (see p. 49). In the years immediately following the king's marriage, Montpensier refused several matches proposed to her by Louis XIV: when she rejected his proposal of King Alfonso VI of Portugal—described by the French envoy in Lisbon as both a stupid drunkard and physically repellent—the king was so displeased that he exiled her once again to Saint-Fargeau. Montpensier returned to the court definitively in 1664, although she was never again as active a participant in its life as she had once been.

At this point, Montpensier seemed destined to live out her life just as she wanted, according to the dreams laid out in the correspondence published

in this volume. Then, suddenly in 1670, the unthinkable happened: Mademoiselle, La Grande Mademoiselle, the king's first cousin and the wealthiest woman in France—fell in love. In her case, love appears to have been even more than usually blind.

According to every rule of the contemporary marriage game, the man she finally decided on was hardly her equal. Antonin Nompar de Caumont, marquis de Puyguilhem, was the third son of the comte de Lauzun, a title he had inherited upon his father's death in 1668. By birth Lauzun was therefore in no way worthy of a member of the royal family; in addition, he was virtually penniless.

Had Montpensier's strange choice turned into a great love match, their union could be celebrated today as the most striking example of a phenomenon documented by historian Carolyn Lougee. During the second half of the seventeenth century, a new view of marriage was promoted both in contemporary novels and in the important seventeenth-century tradition of writing that we would now call feminist, a tradition that, in particular, called for equality between the sexes: marriage was a matter of personal choice and should be based on love, rather than obligation to one's family; a man's personal merit, rather than his social standing or family fortune, should determine a woman's choice of husband. Lougee shows how that view inspired a significant number of women actually to reject all the marital conventions operative in their day and to forge unions with men very clearly their social inferiors. Indeed, as Lougee documents, seventeenth-century France witnessed "a formal celebration of such misalliances." This new type of marriage, based on romantic love and personal merit rather than social standing, was so threatening in Montpensier's day that it contributed in turn to the increasingly widespread opinion that French women with intellectual pretensions, those known in their day as *précieuses*, were deliberately seeking to destabilize French society.[7]

What Montpensier clearly saw as her only chance for happiness within the institution of marriage, marriage revised according to contemporary feminist ideals, was not, however, destined to end, as other contemporary unions apparently did, in storybook fashion. The king at first agreed to the match,

---

7. Carolyn Lougee, *Le Paradis des femmes: Women, Salons, and Social Stratification in Seventeenth-Century France* (Princeton: Princeton University Press, 1976), 49. On the amplitude and the consequences of this phenomenon, see 41–55, 138–70. Patricia Cholakian very convincingly studies Montpensier's involvement with Lauzun as a classic example of the scenario documented by Lougee, in *Women and the Politics of Self-Representation in Seventeenth-Century France* (Newark: University of Delaware Press, 2000), 79–80. On the vision of women as working to corrupt the traditional values of French society, see my *Tender Geographies*, chapter 4.

on December 15, 1670, and Montpensier had already begun, on December 17, the process of raising Lauzun to a more appropriate rank by transferring some of her titles to his name, when her cousin changed his mind and, on December 18, rescinded his permission. A year later the king had Lauzun arrested and imprisoned for ten years in a distant and gloomy fortress at Pignerol. (Louis never justified the arrest, but it seems to have been intended to put an end to Lauzun and Montpensier's protests over his decision to end their engagement.) The king could not have foreseen that Lauzun's captivity would provide in the long run the solution to the problem so many had been seeking to solve for so long, that of gaining control over Montpensier's lands. In order to ransom him, she was forced to give up huge territories—in particular, the earldom of Eu and Dombes, an independent principality that officially became a part of France only in 1762, which she was obliged to sign over to the duc du Maine, the illegitimate son of Louis XIV and Madame de Montespan.

Lauzun was thus allowed to return to Paris. The couple may have been secretly married, though no one is sure that a wedding actually did take place. More important is the fact that the beloved whose freedom she had purchased at such great expense was apparently never even minimally convincing in his declarations of love; he also seems to have paid far too much attention to other women. Montpensier finally simply sent him away, thereby putting a highly unromantic end to her great romance. She continued to work on her memoirs and lived out the last decade of her life quietly at her various estates and, at the end, in the convent of Saint-Séverin in Paris, where she died on April 5, 1693, at age sixty-five.

The folly of Montpensier's choice of Lauzun even today completely distorts the manner in which her biography is usually presented. This one episode is almost invariably put at the center of her life, and virtually all her biographers seem to leap on every occasion to have a laugh at her expense. A great deal is lost because of this distortion. In particular, Montpensier's considerable contributions to the realignment of French literature that took place in the second half of the seventeenth century have been all but forgotten. And the remarkable voice heard in the correspondence that follows, one of the most overtly "feminist" voices of early modern France, has all too rarely been heard.

THE CORRESPONDENCE

In her *Mémoires* Montpensier carefully records the genesis of these letters. It all began with a conversation with her friend Motteville that took place in

Saint-Jean-de-Luz while they were awaiting the royal nuptials. Montpensier, standing at a window gazing out at the Pyrenees, initiated a discussion with Motteville about what life "in complete solitude" would be like, about how one would live if one were able "to live only for oneself." Montpensier then went for a walk along the beach, during which she had the idea for "a project which seemed so extraordinary to me" that she "ran back to her lodgings, took up pen and paper," and immediately dashed off the first letter. Motteville answered, and they continued to exchange letters "over the next year or two" and to develop their plan to establish a community in which a group of noblemen and, above all, noblewomen would live together, "free from the weariness [today we might say 'burnout'] of life at court," creating a world in which marriage and even courtship were banned (C. 3 : 452–54, P. 42 : 490– 91, B. 2 : 146– 47). From their letters we learn that what Montpensier called "solitude" meant not living alone, but living away from the court, while "to live for oneself" signified that one had decided not to marry.

Her correspondent had her own reasons for sharing Montpensier's aversion to marriage. In 1639, when she was eighteen, Françoise Bertaut— daughter of a lady-in-waiting and friend of Louis XIV's mother, Anne of Austria—had been married off to the ninety-year-old Nicolas Langlois, seigneur de Motteville. This union with a wealthy magistrate was considered a good match for the impoverished young woman. Since, however, the marriage had produced no children and the young wife had failed to have any of her husband's assets transferred to her name, she found herself once again in straitened circumstances when she was widowed after only two years of marriage. She was saved from an obligatory second marriage when Anne of Austria, now queen regent, brought her back to court as her lady-in-waiting. Motteville remained in her service, gathering all the while firsthand information on the intrigues of the court, until the queen's death in 1666. From then until her own death in 1689, she lived very quietly in Paris, without contact with the world of influence in which she had spent her entire early life. Of those years we know little, other than that she kept up friendships with literary women, in particular Sévigné and Lafayette. It was then that she put to use her vast knowledge of French political life, when she wrote her *Mémoires pour servir à l'histoire d'Anne d'Autriche, épouse de Louis XIII, roi de France.*[8]

Motteville also had her own reasons for sharing Montpensier's other aversion, to life at court: she and her mother had been sent away from court

8. Motteville's memoirs, once again, were published only in 1723, in the decade following Louis XIV's death. The most readily available edition is in vols. 36– 40 of the series Collection des mémoires relatifs à l'histoire de France, ed. Claude Petitot (Paris: Foucault, 1824–25).

by Richelieu in 1631. From then on she never attempted to play any role more active than that of discreet and disinterested observer of the political scene. Even the memoirs composed at the end of her life, unlike most accounts of the civil war period in France, were those of a passive witness: they are centered not on her personal role, but on Anne of Austria's presence. Motteville played a similar role in her correspondence with Montpensier: she is the ideal sounding board; although she proposes modifications to Montpensier's project, she always makes it clear that Mademoiselle's word is law. Montpensier was clearly the creator of this feminocentric utopia.

Motteville's memoirs contain a decidedly jaundiced view of what she calls "the climate of that country known as the court":

> The air there is gentle and serene for no one. . . . It is a dark zone, full of constant storms. Those who live there . . . are always ill from that contagious disease, ambition, which deprives them of peace and eats away at their heart. . . . This malady also inspires in them a disgust for all the best things in life . . . its sweetness, its innocent pleasures, everything that the wise men of antiquity held in esteem.[9]

The chance encounter at Saint-Jean-de-Luz thus threw together two women all too ready to imagine that life away from "that [dark] country known as the court" could be an idyllic experience, a bucolic retreat sheltered from all the "maladies" of their age.

The life Montpensier imagines for her subjects is reminiscent of the tradition of pastoral poetry that dates back to such classical precursors as Virgil: they will live in harmony with nature, they will dress as shepherdesses, and some of them will even watch over their flocks. Obvious literary references should not, however, lull us into believing that Montpensier intended that her project be absolutely timeless. She calls their community a "Republic," a word the correspondents repeat almost incessantly. That term alone makes us realize that the government of her ideal community would be kinder and gentler than her cousin's monarchy.

The simple fact that Montpensier would have reigned as "sovereign" over their republic also says a great deal: she thereby appropriates for herself a measure of the power that could have been hers in a state without Salic law, the legal code that prevented French princesses from succeeding to the

---

9. This passage, from the first version of Motteville's memoirs—the manuscript of which is found at the Arsenal Library—is not included in all published texts. Petitot cites it in his introduction (36:312–13).

throne and that was often invoked in France to explain cases in which female heirs were pushed aside in favor of their male counterparts. In her memoirs —significantly, in the paragraph immediately following her account of her project for a utopian community—Montpensier comments succinctly on the sphere of women's political influence under French law: "daughters are good for nothing in France" (C. 3:454, P. 42:491, B. 2:147).

The political framework of Montpensier's utopia thus shows us that her project also shares an affinity with a more modern tradition of pastoral literature: from the sixteenth to the eighteenth century, writers all over Europe found the pastoral mode, with its trappings of shepherds and their life of simple innocence, a convenient vehicle for masking political statements that could otherwise have seemed subversive.[10]

Montpensier was naturally well aware of contemporary pastoral literature—witness the prominent reference in her first letter to Honoré d'Urfé's *Astrée* (1607–27), by far the most celebrated French pastoral novel. At the same time, however, she takes exception most violently to the principal pastime in d'Urfé's pastoral fantasy: courtship and romantic love. Seventeenth-century readers would have understood that she was thereby aligning herself with the philosophy of a very particular and today far less known contemporary tradition of utopian writing, one in which a series of French women writers imagined lands or societies under female control. Whether these imaginary realms were situated in ancient Rome or on the plains of Central Asia, whenever women writers imagined countries governed by women, their government was based on two rules: friendship was more important than love, and marriage was either outlawed altogether or else completely redefined so that married women would be legally independent from their husbands.

In this tradition Montpensier's best known precursor was Madeleine de Scudéry, whose novels contain two of the most memorable of these utopias. The final volume of *Artamène, ou Le Grand Cyrus*, published in 1653, features the realm of the Sauromates (according to Herodotus, the land of the Amazons), founded by a group of people exiled after a civil war: it is governed by a queen, and its courts grant legal status to unions outside of marriage, since the society's founding credo, articulated by the volume's central character, Sapho, is that marriage is, in legal terms, "a long slavery" for women

---

10. On the use of the pastoral, particularly in seventeenth-century England, to camouflage dangerous political messages, see Christopher Hill, *Milton and the English Revolution* (New York: Viking, 1978). See Raymond Williams on the early modern revival of the pastoral tradition and for a fascinating reading of the wide range of meanings assigned by different authors to rural life, in *The Country and the City* (London: Chatto and Windus, 1973).

(10:343).[11] A few years later, in the sixth volume of her next novel, *Clélie, histoire romaine*, published in 1658, Scudéry tells the story of "illustrious recluses" ("illustres solitaires") who, tired of "all the world's vanity," have decided to create their own "small world" within "the large one" in order to be able to live in peace. They share a common conviction that friendship is infinitely superior to love (6:1138–45).[12]

Montpensier's contemporaries would thus have recognized the literary context in which she situated her project. Its obvious literary antecedents, and in particular the air of unreality that the pastoral context lends the project—who can really imagine for an instant that the wealthiest woman in Europe would devote herself to watching over a flock of sheep?—should not cause us to forget, however, the concrete, practical details that give Montpensier's project its particular character. She has carefully thought out so many aspects of day-to-day life—the view from the windows of the different houses, the means of transportation available to them, even the games they would play for relaxation—that it is at times easy to think that she was writing the blueprint for a community she believed might one day actually be created. The creative energy of the woman who had used her recent exile to transform a remote and dilapidated country estate into a thriving "ducal" court is everywhere evident. In this regard, we must remember that Montpensier stresses that those who live under her rule will not be exiles, obliged to live in her community: "they will retire from court without having been driven out" (*Mémoires* C. 3:453, P. 42:490, B. 2:146). It is essential to her plan that the new way of life she imagines be freely chosen.

---

11. I cite *Artamène* in the only widely available edition of Scudéry's novel, Editions Slatkine's reprint of its second edition (10 vols.; Geneva: Editions Slatkine, 1973). Scudéry was widely translated in the seventeenth century, but these translations are not readily available today. The Other Voice in Early Modern Europe series recently published *Sapho*, edited and translated by Karen Newman, which contains this feminocentric utopia.

12. I also cite *Clélie* in the Slatkine reprint of the novel's second edition (10 vols.; Geneva: Editions Slatkine, 1973). This particular tradition of utopian speculation did not end with Montpensier's project. Two decades later, for example, Antoinette de Salvan, comtesse de Saliez, began a correspondence with the marquise de Montpelliat in which she developed her plan to found a sect whose members would work to better women's lives—in particular, "by banishing love from our society, lest it should trouble the peace that we are seeking." Their goal was to gain wider acceptance for "equality between the sexes, [which] is no longer questioned among people of quality." *Lettres de Mesdames de Scudéry, de Salvan de Saliez, et de Mlle Descartes* (Paris: Léopold Collin, 1806), 190, 203. In 1704 Salvan de Saliez actually founded an academy, or learned society, based on these principles; it was known as the Chevaliers et Chevalières de la Bonne Foi (xxxvi). Throughout the eighteenth century, French women writers—Françoise de Graffigny and Isabelle de Charrière, for example—continued this tradition of utopian speculation.

To reinforce her point that this is no longer the immediate post-Fronde era, Montpensier carefully dates two key letters, a decision that no longer seems noteworthy today but was just that in her day. The vast majority of the letters that have survived from the first half of the seventeenth century are not dated; the years in which Montpensier began her correspondence mark the moment when dating letters began to be standard practice. That custom was part of a major shift in epistolary practice, away from what are known as public letters—missives intended from the start for publication, as part of letter manuals, as rhetorical exercises, or as contributions to a polemic (many political tracts printed during the Fronde took the form of letters, for example)—in the direction of the more private circulation of letters that we now take for granted. For, whereas public letters were almost never dated, private correspondence generally was.

Even though Montpensier realized the likelihood that these letters would be made public, those two strategically placed dates signal her desire to commemorate the correspondence's origin in an exchange of personal letters. The dates also reveal her wish to guarantee that her readers remain conscious of the precise historical context in which her project unfolded. In this way, the initial letter's relation to the upcoming royal marriage becomes unmistakable. In similar fashion, Montpensier's final letter is just as precisely situated: "Forges, the first of August 1661." Montpensier concluded their correspondence when she was in another type of retreat from the court, at the spa town of Forges, where she had retired to take the waters. She ironically compares the people in various states of ill health with whom she finds herself surrounded there to the group she had hoped to gather together in a country retreat, thereby making clear her awareness of the way the political climate was changing around her. She was correct in her evaluation, for those changes would put an end to any type of active involvement on the part of women, such as the community she had envisioned.

In August 1661 the French monarchy was about to enter a new age. On March 9 of that year, Cardinal Mazarin died. At that point Louis XIV decided that he would rule alone, without the type of all-powerful minister on whom first his father and then his mother had relied. The month following Montpensier's last letter, the new reign began in earnest when Louis had his most powerful rival for influence over policy in France, Finance Minister Nicolas Fouquet, arrested and imprisoned. The new spirit of absolutism meant in effect that the time was over when one might take seriously the notion of "a corner of the world in which . . . women are their own mistresses," as Montpensier so proudly proclaims at the close of the third letter of her correspondence with Motteville.

In 1661 the king celebrated his new independence by beginning work on a project of his own, the reconstruction of Versailles, the château that would come to be seen as the ultimate monument to his absolutism. With Versailles, Louis guaranteed in particular that the principal members of the French aristocracy henceforth would all be kept together in one community and under one roof, perpetually under the king's surveillance. Nobles would never again gather together out of their monarch's sight. When she dates her final letter, Montpensier can be seen as signifying her awareness that, just as the days of Amazonian political activity were irrevocably past, it was also too late for the other new dreams for women to which her project stands as a blueprint.

In the manuscript I consulted for this edition, the letters are followed by "The Story of Princesse Adamirze," a short story three times as long as the correspondence to which it is appended. The fiction's author is never identified; Motteville explains that she is sending it to Montpensier to show her that she is not the first great princess "who desired the solitary life": even though Princess Adamirze lived in ancient Persia, "her life can be compared to [yours]." Indeed, the story that follows—of a princess who chose to live her life far from the court and to establish "a republic and a society of nobles" to which women flocked since its customs were so much more favorable to them than those established by Persian law—reproduces all the key elements of Montpensier's utopia.

The story, allegedly translated from Persian by a French scholar, is a very early example of a type of fiction soon to become enormously popular in France and referred to either as an oriental tale or a fairy tale (even though, as is the case here, fairies do not always put in an appearance). In this example the characters do not live "happily ever after"—or at least not in the manner traditional to fairy tales. The emperor of Persia, who has done all he can, despite many rejections, to convince the princess to marry him, is killed. Adamirze lives out her long life—happy and fulfilled—in her feminist republic.[13]

Motteville includes the date on which she sent the tale: 1664, the year Montpensier was allowed to return to court after her second exile. It was as if she had decided to use the Persian princess's story to reinforce Montpensier's resolution to remain aloof from court life and its marital politics. This seemingly contradictory blend—a fairy tale bearing a historical inscription —is appropriate for Montpensier's feminocentric utopia, which exists in

---

13. Because the "fairy tale" is so long and its authorship uncertain, I chose not to translate it for this volume.

similar fashion on the border between real life and fantasy. I have already stressed the aspects of fantasy, so I will close on two ways in which the project mapped out a plan of action that could be termed realistic: Montpensier's vision of socially responsible rural life and her hopes for women's intellectual achievements.

The correspondence seems in many ways to announce the eighteenth-century English tradition of speculation on how life on the great country estates could be made responsive to the needs of the people who worked the land, how it could function in opposition to the new, proto-capitalist economic forces that were seen as having corrupted the contemporary city.[14] In this respect, Montpensier's project is a far cry from the well-known French tradition of pastoral as escapist aristocratic entertainment, a tradition whose most visible proponent was undoubtedly Queen Marie Antoinette, playing milkmaid in her pseudo-rustic cottage at Versailles even as the forces that led to the Revolution of 1789 were gathering. Montpensier's pastoral vision has, on the contrary, a solid social base—note in particular the conclusion to her opening letter, in which she makes provisions for a hospital where the poor would receive medical care, as well as for an institution where poor children would be fed and taught a trade. Here, Montpensier is calling for a type of Christian charity, a value promoted among aristocratic women in her day, when for the first time ever they were actively encouraged to visit the sick, for example, or to give alms to the poor.

The provision Montpensier makes for a moral community is one of the key means she would use to replace romantic love. In addition, Montpensier's humanitarianism, her emphasis on a virtuous and responsible life, lays the foundation for what can be seen as a new feudal order, one that could have served as a replacement for the old order her cousin was about to begin dismantling when he forced the French nobility to abandon their landed estates and move to Versailles. In her republic her subjects would, as lords had traditionally done, provide for those who lived on their land. Unlike that of their precursors, however, their rule would be founded on social and economic bonds, rather than on military and physical control. With this proposal, Montpensier thereby aligned herself with the tradition of progressive thinkers who, from the late seventeenth century on, sought to devise ways of reversing the continuing deterioration in relations between aristocrats and peasants that clouded the last century of the French monarchy.

14. For more on this English tradition of commentary on rural life, see Williams, *The Country and the City*, chapter 3.

Montpensier's project was progressive in a second way, one closer to our concerns today. All the residences in her republic were to contain both libraries and studies, places in which literary creation could take place. She was sure, moreover, that this would be the case: "I have no doubt that we would have among us some who would also write books," she announces in her first letter (see p. 31). Like Virginia Woolf nearly three centuries later, Montpensier—who, you will remember, had just used her years of enforced exile to become a published author—clearly understood that "a woman must have money and a room of her own if she is to write fiction." She also shared Woolf's understanding that marriage had traditionally been an obstacle to women's creativity because upon her marriage a woman lost the legal control over her property.[15]

It is, of course, in a way impossible to compare the sense of economic reality possessed by the wealthiest woman in Europe with Woolf's modest dreams of a private room and sufficient funds to scrape by on. And yet in the exalted cry with which Montpensier ends her third letter—"let there be a corner of the world in which it can be said that women are their own mistresses . . . ; and let us celebrate ourselves for the centuries to come"—we hear precisely the kind of enabling voice that Woolf looked for in the long history of women's writing.[16] In the end, both realized that spatial independence, the possibility of a place where "women are their own mistresses," was of the essence if women were to leave a permanent legacy.

When she reflected on this correspondence in her memoirs, Montpensier concluded that "if both sides of the correspondence were gathered together, there would be enough to fill a small volume" (C. 3:453, P. 42:490, B. 2:147). Nearly three and a half centuries later, this thinly veiled request to make fully public her dreams for all that women might accomplish if they were allowed to rule over "a corner of the world" is at last being answered.

A NOTE ON THE FRENCH TEXT

The title page of the manuscript on which the present edition is based tells us that among Montpensier's contemporaries, these letters were "famous on account of the acclaim they had received at the court and in Paris." This

---

15. Virginia Woolf, *A Room of One's Own* (1929; New York: Harcourt Brace Jovanovich, 1957), 4, 116.

16. "Moreover, if you consider any great figure of the past, like Sappho, like the Lady Murasaki, like Emily Brontë, you will find that she is an inheritor as well as an originator" (Woolf, *Room of One's Own*, 113).

indicates that the correspondence circulated widely in manuscript. The first four of these letters have been published several times in volumes that gather together various kinds of letters, first in 1667 and most recently in 1806. All subsequent editions follow the 1667 text. In her *Mémoires* Montpensier writes that she did not authorize this edition: she adds that the four letters had been so "mangled" that she considered them "ruined" (C. 3:454, P. 42:491, B. 2:147). For this edition I followed the text of a manuscript recently acquired by the Bibliothèque nationale de France: NAF 25670. The manuscript gives a version of the first four letters substantially different from that found in earlier editions. Furthermore, the manuscript contains the text of four additional letters, published here for the first time. We know that the correspondence as published in the 1667 edition was incomplete: in her *Mémoires* Montpensier says that they exchanged letters "for a year or two" (C. 3:453, P. 42:491, B. 2:146). This corresponds to the time frame of the eight letters found in the Bibliothèque nationale's manuscript, which were written over a period of some fifteen months, and which, unlike the first four letters that end in medias res, form a complete unit.

While the manuscript followed here is not an autograph manuscript, it is in a late-seventeenth-century hand. We know that Montpensier had copies made of her works—her *Mémoires*, in particular—that she presented to her friends. It is not unlikely that the Bibliothèque nationale's manuscript is one such copy, that it therefore gives us our first access ever to the correspondence as it was written.

The French text published here follows the manuscript almost to the letter. I respected its use of capitals: we know that these were considered a way of emphasizing a word's importance; they are thus a trace of the correspondence's orality, an essential quality in a text whose tone is overwhelmingly conversational. Nothing signals that orality more clearly than the manuscript's punctuation. Both women favor the long, loose sentences typical of the French prose of their day. Readers today, who know seventeenth-century prose only from modern editions—all of which radically modernize its punctuation—may be surprised by their sentences. I suggest reading at least some of the letters aloud to get a sense of the conversational flow and oral qualities of this prose.[17] In the self-portrait she contributed to the portrait collection she edited in 1659, Montpensier remarks, "I write well, freely

---

17. For an explanation of why many editors are now reproducing the use of capitals in early modern publications, see Roger Chartier, *Publishing Drama in Early Modern Europe* (London: British Museum, 1999), 20. On the manner in which the original punctuation of seventeenth-century prose contributes to its oral quality, see Bernard Bray's edition of Tristan L'Hermite's *Œuvres complètes* (Paris: Honoré Champion, 1999), 1:70.

and in a natural style."[18] In this correspondence the original punctuation brings us closer to that "free, natural style." I made very few changes in the original punctuation; they are indicated by means of brackets. I also standardized two practices irregularly used in the manuscript: capital letters to begin each sentence and commas around forms of address such as "illustrious princess."

A NOTE ON THE TRANSLATION

In the English translation, I modified the highly oral style of this correspondence in one major way, by breaking down many of the very long sentences into shorter units. I often inserted a sentence break where an extended phrase in the French text begins with a "but"; in these cases I usually changed the "but" to a "however." Otherwise, I tried to preserve as much of the rhythm of their exchange as possible.

18. Vita Sackville-West includes a translation of Montpensier's self-portrait in her highly readable and informative biography, *Daughter of France: The Life of La Grande Mademoiselle* (Garden City, N.Y.: Doubleday, 1959), 177–78. Christian Bouyer gives the French text in a recent reedition of part of her portrait collection: Anne-Marie-Louise d'Orléans, duchesse de Montpensier, *Portraits littéraires*, ed. Christian Bouyer (Paris: Séguier, 2000), 23–27. See Cholakian, *Women and the Politics of Self-Representation*, 67, for a discussion of the "conversational style" of the autograph manuscript of Montpensier's *Mémoires* and the manner in which this style was made more conventional in the manuscript as recopied by her secretary.

MONTPENSIER-MOTTEVILLE
CORRESPONDANCE

Lettres de Mademoiselle écrites à Madame de Motteville, fameuses par l'approbation qu'elles reçurent à la Cour et à Paris; et ses Réponses à cette Princesse.

LETTRE 1
Lettre de Mademoiselle à

Madame de Motteville à Saint-Jean-de-Luz sur une conversation qu'elle eut l'honneur de faire avec elle à la vue de la mer sur le bonheur de la vie solitaire envoyée par un homme inconnu.

A Saint-Jean-de-Luz le 14 mai 1660

M'étant trouvée l'autre jour auprès de vous lorsque vous causiez chez la Reine avec une de vos amies du bonheur de la vie retirée, il me sembla que votre conversation n'avait jamais été plus charmante et plus agréable, je l'écoutais avec plaisir, et depuis j'ai passé de bonnes heures à y penser, ce lieu étant le plus propre du monde à entretenir la rêverie lors qu'on se promène sur le bord de la mer; ainsi, Madame, je me suis imaginée que vous ne trouveriez pas mauvais que je vous fisse part des sentiments que vous m'avez inspirés et de l'opinion que j'estime qu'il faut avoir pour rendre cette retraite dont vous parliez, divertissante et profitable. Premièrement, Madame, il faudrait à mon avis que les personnes qui voudraient se retirer de la cour ou du monde s'éloignassent de l'un et de l'autre sans en être rebutées, mais par la connaissance du peu de solidité qu'on trouve dans ce commerce et même parmi ses amis. Il y a eu de fort honnêtes gens de tout sexe qui n'ayant pas eu autant d'habitudes que vous et moi à la Cour ont pu néanmoins s'en éloigner par le mépris de la fortune, et il est aisé de ne s'en pas soucier quand on est parvenu par ses soins ou par sa naissance à en avoir une honnête selon sa condition; on peut aussi se trouver en âge où l'ambition est moins vive et où les personnes fort raisonnables peuvent s'en guérir facilement, car je tiens qu'il y a des temps qu'il serait aussi peu honnête d'en être tourmenté

MONTPENSIER-MOTTEVILLE
CORRESPONDENCE

The letters of Mademoiselle written to Madame de Motteville, famous on account of the acclaim they received at the court and in Paris; and her replies to this princess.

LETTER 1

A letter, dispatched by an unknown man, from Mademoiselle to Madame de Motteville at Saint-Jean-de-Luz concerning a conversation that she had the honor of having with her, while looking out over the sea, on the happiness of a solitary life.

Saint-Jean-de-Luz, May 14, 1660

Finding myself next to you the other day at the queen's when you were speaking with one of your friends about the joys of the secluded life, I thought that your conversation had never been more charming and agreeable. I listened with pleasure and since then I have spent many hours thinking about it, this place being the most conducive in the world to foster day dreaming while one walks by the sea. Thus, Madame, I thought that you would not think it amiss of me to share with you the feelings you inspired in me, as well as the principles that I consider necessary to make the seclusion that you were discussing both entertaining and beneficial. In the first place, Madame, it is essential, in my opinion, that the people who would like to withdraw from the court or from society distance themselves from those places without feeling obliged to leave them,[1] but rather because they are aware of how little constancy can be found in this type of life and even among

---

1. The French phrase "sans en être rebutées" could be translated somewhat more literally as "without having been put off or repelled by them." In her discussion of this correspondence's genesis in her memoirs, however, Montpensier—whose long political exile after the Fronde was still fresh in her mind in 1660—makes it clear that she means a voluntary decision to leave the court, rather than an officially decreed departure, so I chose a translation with a harder edge.

qu'il l'aurait été de s'y être toujours montré insensible. Comme on doit faire ce raisonnement en toutes sortes de conditions, et qu'il est comme vous savez des héros et des héroïnes de toute manière, aussi nous faut-il de toutes sortes de personnes pour pouvoir parler de toutes choses dans la conversation, qui à votre goût et au mien est le plus grand plaisir de la vie, et presque le seul à mon gré: néanmoins j'opinerais assez qu'il n'y eût point de gens mariés et que ce fussent toutes personnes veuves, ou qui eussent renoncé à ce sacrement, car on dit que c'est un embarquement fâcheux, vous savez si l'on est heureuse d'en être dehors. Pour moi je décide là-dessus d'une manière que ceux qui ne me connaîtront point ne devineront pas qui je suis par ce que j'en dis. Il serait bon de concerter tous ensemble du lieu de l'habitation et de délibérer si on choisirait les bords de la Loire ou ceux de la Seine, quelques-uns aimeraient les bords de la mer, pour moi qui n'aime pas naturellement l'eau, j'aimerais la vue de la mer et des rivières un peu en éloignement, et que ma maison fût située dans le voisinage d'un grand bois, que l'on y arrivât par de grandes routes où le soleil se ferait voir à peine en plein midi; je la bâtirais de la plus agréable manière que je pourrais l'imaginer, les dedans seraient de même, propres et point magnifiques non plus que les meubles, car il ne convient point quand on méprise tout et que l'on veut paraître au-dessus de toutes choses, d'avoir la faiblesse de s'attacher à la superfluité. Je voudrais que cette maison fût environnée de jardins, et que le terroir en fût propre à produire les plus excellents fruits. Je prendrais un grand plaisir à faire planter et à voir croître tous ces arbres différents; s'il y avait de quoi faire des fontaines je n'en serais pas fâchée, mais j'aimerais mieux la vue que l'eau, pour mieux dire chacun ferait bâtir sa maison à sa fantaisie, les uns dans le fond d'un bois, les autres au bord de la rivière. La situation que je choisis pour moi laisse de quoi choisir à tous les autres, parce qu'au bas de la côte où je m'imagine cette belle forêt et d'où l'on pourrait se faire une si belle vue je prétends qu'il y aurait de grandes prairies et qu'elles seraient coupées de ruisseaux d'une eau claire et vive qui en serpentant sur l'herbe irait gagner la rivière. On se visiterait à cheval, en calèche ou avec des chaises roulantes, quelquefois à pied, quelquefois en carosse, si ce n'est que je pense que peu en auraient[.] Le soin d'ajuster sa maison et son jardin occuperait beaucoup, ceux qui aiment la vie active travailleraient à toutes sortes d'ouvrages, ou s'amuseraient à peindre ou à dessiner, et les paresseux entretiendraient ceux qui s'occuperaient de la sorte. Je pense qu'on lirait beaucoup et qu'il n'y aurait personne qui n'eût sa bibliothèque. On ne romprait point le commerce qu'on aurait avec ses amis de la Cour et du monde, mais je pense que nous pourrions croire qu'il leur serait plus glorieux de nous écrire qu'à nous de leur faire réponse. Je me

one's friends. There have been people of the highest rank[2] of both sexes who, not having been as accustomed to the court as you and I, were nonetheless able to distance themselves from it because of their scorn for fortune, and it is easy not to worry about the court when one has managed, through one's efforts or birth, to have a fortune commensurate with one's station. One can also find oneself at an age when ambition is less compelling and when reasonable people are easily cured of it, for I believe that there are times when it would be as indecent to be tormented by it as it would be always to have appeared to be unaffected by it. Since those of very different conditions also feel this way, and since there are, as you know, heroes and heroines of all sorts, so too do we need all kinds of people so that we can talk about all subjects when we converse, an activity that, to your taste and mine, is the greatest pleasure in life, and almost the only one I enjoy. Nevertheless, I would rather there were no married people and that everyone would either be widowed, or have renounced this sacrament, for it is said to be an unfortunate undertaking. You know how lucky we are to be out of it. For my part, in this matter I have come to this decision in such a way that those who do not know me will not guess who I am by what I say about it. It would be good to come to an absolute agreement about the place where we would live and to consider whether we would choose the banks of the Loire or those of the Seine. Some would like the seashore; since I am not, by nature, drawn to water, I would prefer to view the sea and rivers from somewhat of a distance, and for my house to be located near a large forest, for it to be reached by wide roads where the sun would barely show itself, even at noon. I would build it in the most pleasant way I could imagine, the inside would be the same, neat and simple like the furniture, for when one scorns everything and wants to appear above it all, one should not succumb to the weakness of extravagance. I would like this house to be surrounded by gardens, and the soil to be suitable for growing the most excellent fruit. I would take great pleasure in having all sorts of different trees planted and in watching them grow; if it were possible to create fountains, I would not be displeased, but I would prefer to have a nice view than the water necessary for them. To explain it better, each person would have their house built according to their tastes, some in the heart of the forest, others on the banks of the river. The location that I would

2. The French phrase is "honnêtes gens": "honnête" is both among the most frequently used adjectives in seventeenth-century French prose from this period and one of the most difficult to translate. It has meanings ranging from "of noble birth" to "courteous," "cultured," "virtuous," "decent," even "reasonable."

persuade que dans ce bois ou dans quelque belle allée il y aurait un jeu de mail;[1] c'est un jeu honnête et un exercice convenable à la santé du corps qu'il est bon de ne pas négliger en songeant à celle de l'esprit. On nous enverrait tous les livres nouveaux, tous les vers, et ceux qui les auraient les premiers auraient une grande joie d'en aller faire part aux autres. Je ne doute point que nous n'eussions parmi nous des personnes qui mettraient aussi quelques ouvrages en lumière chacun selon son talent, puisqu'il n'y a personne qui n'en ait un tout à fait dissemblable quand on veut suivre son naturel. Ceux qui aimeraient la musique la pourraient entendre, puisque nous aurions parmi nous des personnes qui auraient la voix belle et qui chanteraient bien, d'autres qui joueraient du Luth, du Clavecin et des plus agréables instruments. Les violons se sont rendus si communs que sans avoir beaucoup de domestiques, chacun en ayant quelques-uns auxquels il aurait fait apprendre il y aurait moyen de faire une bonne bande quand ils seraient tous assemblés. Je ne trouverais point à redire que lorsque l'on serait obligé d'aller à la Cour ou aux grandes villes, soit pour affaires ou pour rendre quelque devoir de parenté, on ne s'en dispensât point. Je ne voudrais pas que l'on fît les farouches en disant je ne veux assister à nulle fête, je ne ferais pas une visite pour mourir, et quand j'y serais je voudrais m'accommoder aux autres et me rendre commode. Néanmoins je crois que je m'ennuierais fort, et que j'aurais grande joie de retourner, mais je ne le témoignerais pas de crainte que cette affectation ne me fît haïr, ou ne m'exposât à la raillerie d'autant plus dangereuse qu'elle est bien fondée et qu'on se l'attire par des façons ridicules. Comme les personnes du monde se déguisent présentement et que cette façon de faire qui n'était point bienséante aux gens de condition autrefois s'est maintenant mise en usage[,] je ne désapprouverais point que parmi nous on prît aussi quelquefois ce divertissement mais d'une manière moins folle. Je voudrais que l'on allât garder les troupeaux de moutons dans ces belles prairies, qu'on eût des houlettes et des capelines, qu'on dinât sur l'herbe verte de mets rustiques et convenables aux bergers, et qu'on imitât quelquefois ce qu'on a lu dans *l'Astrée* sans toutefois faire l'amour, car cela ne me plaît point en quelque habit que ce soit; lorsqu'on serait revêtu de celui de berger je ne

---

1.   The game known in French as "mail" or "pale-mail" became popular in Italy and France in the sixteenth century and in England in the seventeenth: it had characteristics of the French game of *boules* and others of croquet. The objective was to drive a metal-tipped boxwood ball through an iron ring suspended above the ground at the end of a long alley known as a "mail."

choose for myself would leave a great deal of choice to all the others, because at the bottom of the slope, where I imagine this beautiful forest to be and from which one could have such a beautiful view, I envision large meadows crisscrossed by streams of clear, rushing water, which, snaking through the grass, would empty into the river. We would visit each other on horseback, in carriages, or in bath chairs, sometimes on foot, sometimes in coaches, though I think that few would have the latter. The business of setting up one's house and garden would occupy many; those who like an active life would work at all sorts of tasks, or would amuse themselves by painting or drawing; and those who didn't want to engage in such activities would keep the others company. I think that we would read a good deal and there would be no one without a library. We would not break off the commerce we have with our friends at the court and in society, but I think we can be sure that it would be more glorious for them to write to us than for us to answer them. I am certain that in this forest or in some lovely lane, there would be a pall-mall court;[3] it is a worthy game and a fitting exercise for the health of the body, which we would do well not to neglect at the expense of that of the mind. We would be sent all the latest books, and all the poetry, and those who received them first would take great pleasure in sharing them with others. I have no doubt that we would have among us some who would also write books, each according to her talent, since we all have unique talents if we follow our own instincts. Those who like music would be able to listen to it, since we would have among us people who would have beautiful voices and who would sing well, others who would play the lute, the harpsichord, and the most pleasing instruments. Even though none of us would have a large number of servants, each of us would have a few who could play that most common of instruments, the violin, so that we would be able to form a good orchestra when they were all gathered together. I would not find fault with those who, when forced to go to the court or a large city, either for business or for reasons of family, would not excuse themselves from going. I would not want us to be unsociable, saying that we do not want to go to any gatherings, that we would rather die than go visiting, and when I was engaged in social events, I would hope that I would adapt myself to others and be agreeable. Nonetheless, I believe that I would be bored and that I would be very happy to

3. The game known in French as "mail" or "pale-mail" became popular in Italy and France in the sixteenth century and in England in the seventeenth: it had characteristics of the French game of *boules* and others of croquet. The objective was to drive a metal-tipped boxwood ball through an iron ring suspended above the ground at the end of a long alley known as a "mail."

désapprouverais pas qu'on tirât ses vaches ni que l'on fît des fromages et des gâteaux, puisqu'il faut manger et que je ne prétends pas que le plan de notre vie soit fabuleux comme ces Romans où l'on observe un jeûne perpétuel et une si sévère abstinence, je voudrais au contraire qu'on pût n'avoir rien de mortel que de manger, mais il faut finir par ce qui doit être la fin de toutes choses. Après avoir beaucoup rêvé sur le bonheur de la vie, après avoir lu exactement l'histoire de tous les temps, examiné les mœurs et la différence de tous les pays, la vie des plus grands Héros et des plus parfaites Héroïnes et des plus sages philosophes de tous les siècles passés, je ne trouve personne en tout cela qui ait été parfaitement heureux, et j'ai remarqué que ceux qui n'ont point connu le Christianisme le cherchaient sans y penser, ils ont été fort raisonnables et sans savoir ce qui leur manquait ils s'apercevaient bien qu'il leur manquait quelque chose. J'ai remarqué aussi que ceux qui l'ayant connu, l'ont méprisé, et n'ont pas suivi ses préceptes ont été malheureux ou en leurs personnes ou en leurs Etats, qu'il est difficile enfin de faire rien de bon sans songer à sa fin: la nôtre doit être notre salut, ainsi toutes personnes y doivent penser. Je voudrais que dans notre désert[2] il y eût un couvent de Carmélites et qu'elles n'excédassent point le nombre que Sainte Thérèse marque dans sa régle; son intention était qu'elles fussent ermites, et le séjour des ermites est dans les bois, leur bâtiment serait fait sur celui d'Avila qui fut le premier. La vie d'ermite nous empêcherait d'avoir un commerce trop fréquent avec elles, mais plus elles seraient retirées du commerce du monde plus nous aurions de vénération pour elles. Ce serait dans leur Eglise qu'on irait prier Dieu; comme il y aurait d'habiles Docteurs retirés dans notre désert on ne manquerait pas d'excellents sermons, ceux qui les aimeraient iraient plus souvent, et les autres moins, sans être contraints dans sa dévotion. J'approuverais fort aussi qu'il y eût une belle Eglise servie par des prêtres séculiers, habiles et zélés, et qui iraient instruire les villages voisins, je ne voudrais pas néanmoins qu'ils préchassent sans mission, car j'aime l'ordre en toutes choses. Je voudrais que nous eussions un hôpital où l'on nourrirait des pauvres Enfants, où on leur ferait apprendre des métiers, et où l'on recevrait les malades, on se divertirait à voir travailler les uns et l'on s'occuperait à servir les autres. Enfin je voudrais que rien ne nous manquât pour mener une vie parfaitement morale et chrétienne de laquelle

---

2. In the seventeenth century, "désert" could be used to refer to a spiritual retreat; an isolated country retreat was also referred to as a "désert."

return home, but I would not let it show for fear that this affectation would make others despise me, or would expose me to a mockery all the more dangerous because it is well founded and that it is brought on by ridiculous behavior. Because worldly people put on disguises today and this fashion that was not fitting for people of quality in times past has of late become common, I would not disapprove if among us we sometimes indulged in this amusement, though in less extravagant fashion. I would like us to keep herds of sheep in these beautiful meadows, to have shepherds' staffs and wide-brimmed hats, to sit down on the green grass and to dine on rustic fare like that of shepherds, and sometimes to imitate what we have read in *L'Astrée* though without amorous pursuit, for that does not please me in any guise. When we are wearing shepherds' clothing, I would not disapprove of those who milk the cows nor of those who make cheeses and cakes, since we must eat, and I do not propose that the project for our life should be as far-fetched as those novels where they observe a perpetual fast and rigorous abstinence is practiced. I would want eating to be our only activity related to concerns of the flesh, but we must end as all things necessarily end. After having given much thought to the happiness of life, having carefully read the history of all periods, and studied the customs and the characteristics of each country, the lives of the greatest heroes and the most perfect heroines and the wisest philosophers of all the past centuries, in all that, I found no one who was perfectly happy, and I noticed that those who were not familiar with Christianity were looking for it without knowing it; they clearly perceived that, while they did not know what they were lacking, something was missing. I also noticed that those who, once acquainted with it, disdained it and did not follow its precepts were unhappy either in their persons or their states, and that, in the end, it is difficult to do anything good without keeping one's purpose in mind: ours should be our salvation; thus, we should all think about it. I would like there to be a convent of Carmelites in our wilderness,[4] not exceeding the number that Saint Teresa established in her regulations. She intended for them to be hermits, and the abode of hermits is in the woods. Their convent would be built on the model of the one in Avila, which was the first. Their hermit's life would keep us from having much contact with them, but the more distanced from the business of the world they would be, the more we would admire them. It would be in their church that we would pray to God. Since able theologians would retire to our retreat, we would never want for

---

4. The French word is "desert." In the seventeenth century, the word could be used to refer to a spiritual retreat; an isolated country estate was also referred to as a "desert."

les plaisirs innocents ne sont point bannis, au contraire on peut dire que c'est là qu'on les goûte véritablement[.]

Mademoiselle de Vandy après avoir entendu lire ce que Mademoiselle avait écrit y ajouta cette dernière ligne comme un défi qu'elle fit.

Devine si tu peux, et réponds si tu l'oses.[3]

LETTRE 2

Madame de Motteville
à Mademoiselle

Il est juste, Illustre Princesse, que vos idées surpassent les miennes, que leur perfection et leur beauté conviennent à la hauteur de votre naissance et que toutes les productions de votre esprit nous marquent en toutes choses la différence qui est entre vous et les autres personnes de votre sexe. Selon l'inclination que j'ai toujours eue d'estimer la solitude, j'ai cru que les bois, les prés les ruisseaux et les rivières qui formeraient un agréable désert seraient une délicieuse retraite, j'ai souvent pensé que les personnes raisonnables qui connaîtraient assez le monde pour le mépriser seraient heureuses de le quitter pour vivre d'une vie innocente, éloignée des occasions qui corrompent

---

3. The letter's close refers to the fiction Montpensier adopted when she initiated the correspondence: Motteville was obliged to guess the identity of her "unknown" correspondent in order to respond. Catherine d'Aspremont, known as Mademoiselle de Vandy, was often a member of Montpensier's entourage, beginning with her exile at Saint-Fargeau. The sentence also refers to a line from Pierre Corneille's 1646–47 tragedy, *Héraclius, empereur d'Orient*: "Devine, si tu peux, et choisis, si tu l'oses" (IV:iv:1408).

excellent sermons: those who like sermons would hear them more often, and the others less, without anyone being constrained in their worship. I would also be very pleased to have a beautiful church staffed by capable and zealous clerics who would teach in the neighboring villages; nonetheless, I would not want them to preach without a calling, for I like order in all things. I would like us to have a hospital where poor children would be fed, where they would be taught trades, and where sick people would be taken in. We would enjoy watching some of them work and would occupy ourselves with serving the others. Last of all, I would not want anything to be missing that would allow us to lead a perfectly moral and Christian life, where innocent pleasures would not be banished; on the contrary, it can be said that these could be truly enjoyed in such an environment.

Mademoiselle de Vandy after having heard read what Mademoiselle had written, added this last line as a challenge:

Guess if you can, and answer if you dare.[5]

LETTER 2

Madame de Motteville
to Mademoiselle

It is only just, illustrious Princess, that your ideas should surpass mine, that their perfection and beauty are worthy of the nobility of your birth, and that all the products of your mind prove to us the difference that exists in every domain between you and the other members of your sex. Because of the inclination toward solitude that I have always had, I believe that the woods, the meadows, the streams, and the rivers that would make a pleasant wilderness would be a delicious retreat. I have often thought that sensible people who knew the world enough to disdain it would be happy to leave it for a simple life, far away from the events that corrupt morals, and living in accor-

5. The letter's close refers to the fiction Montpensier adopted when she initiated the correspondence: Motteville was obliged to guess the identity of her "unknown" correspondent in order to respond. Catherine d'Aspremont, known as Mademoiselle de Vandy, was often a member of Montpensier's entourage, beginning with her exile at Saint-Fargeau. The sentence also refers to a line from Pierre Corneille's 1646–47 tragedy, *Héraclius, empereur d'Orient:* "Guess, if you can, and choose, if you dare" (IV : iv : 1408).

les mœurs, et soumise aux divines loix de l'Evangile. J'ai souvent cherché les moyens de joindre à la pieté chrétienne la sagesse des philosophes, et la politesse des fabuleux bergers de Lignon,[4] mais, belle Amelinte, je n'aurais jamais cru qu'on pût perfectionner cette sorte de vie au point que vous avez fait, et qu'on pût assembler tant de contraires ensemble; vous y avez introduit des calèches et vous ne voulez garder les brebis que par divertissement. Je vois bien ce que c'est, vous êtes née pour commander et pour porter des couronnes, et il est si raisonnable que cela soit ainsi que je ne m'étonne pas de ce que sans y penser vous vous êtes établie notre Souveraine. Cette puissance, Grande Princesse, vous est légitimement due, d'autres élévations vous attendent et vous pouvez choisir dans l'Europe les peuples qu'il vous plaira de commander, mais si votre philosophie vous convie à choisir nos bois plutôt qu'un Empire, je suis assurée que la félicité de vos solitaires sujets sera si grande que tous les Rois du monde auront sujet de les envier[.] Vous ferez honte à ces Législateurs qui ont donné des Lois aux Grecs et aux Romains; ces illustres sages n'ont établi que la fausse sagesse et n'ont gouverné que des peuples abandonnés à la volupté et à tous les dérèglements que le Paganisme pur permettait; mais les vôtres sont beaucoup plus parfaites, elles bannissent les passions, ordonnent la pratique de la vertu et font régner l'innocence même dans les plaisirs: c'est pourquoi nous nous y soumettons volontiers, et vous supplions de nous commander et de nous conduire dans le chemin de la sagesse; mais comme il est de l'ordre de la raison que les Inférieurs vivent différemment de leurs Souverains, nous choisissons d'être toujours bergères, et d'avoir pour principale occupation de garder nos troupeaux, parce que nous croyons que la longue habitude à la vie solitaire nous fera acquérir ce que vous possédez naturellement, nous donnera de l'esprit et de la lumière, nous élevera l'âme à la contemplation des choses célestes et nous rendra dignes d'être gouvernées par la plus grande princesse du monde[.] Nos premiers pères qui étaient eux-mêmes de grands princes n'ont pas méprisé cette occupation, et le soin de leurs troupeaux ne les a pas empêchés de pénétrer jusque dans les cieux et de méditer les premiers sur les différents effets des étoiles. C'est pourquoi nous tiendrons à gloire de leur ressembler et d'enrichir notre simplicité des plus estimables trésors de la vie. Nous ne voulons que de petites cabanes dont nous bannirons le magnifique et où nous ne voulons souffrir que le nécessaire, chacun de nous choisira la situation du lieu de sa demeure selon son inclination particulière, et comme vous préférez la vue aux autres beautés de la campagne, je souhaiterais pour la mienne l'obscurité d'un bois

---

4. "The shepherds of Lignon" are characters in Honoré d'Urfé's novel *L'Astrée.*

dance with the divine laws of the Gospel. I have often looked for ways to bring together the wisdom of the philosophers and Christian piety, as well as the politeness of the marvelous shepherds of Lignon.[6] However, beautiful Amelinte, I would never have thought it possible to perfect this type of life to the extent that you have, or to bring together so many opposites: you have introduced carriages, and you only watch over your sheep to pass the time. I see clearly how it is: you were born to rule and to wear a crown, and it is so logical for things to be this way that I am not surprised that, without even giving it a second thought, you have established yourself as our sovereign. This power, noble Princess, is rightly your due; other honors await you, and you could choose to rule any of the peoples of Europe, but if your philosophy induces you to choose our forest rather than an empire, I am sure that the bliss of your isolated subjects will be so great that all the kings in the world will have reason to envy them. You will put to shame the legislators who gave the Greeks and Romans their laws; those illustrious sages taught only false wisdom and governed only subjects who had abandoned themselves to debauchery and to all the disorders that pure paganism permits. Your laws are much more perfect: they banish passions, prescribe the observance of virtue, and make innocence reign even among pleasure: that is why we submit ourselves to them voluntarily, and we implore you to rule over us and to lead us in the path of wisdom. But as it is right that subjects live differently from their sovereign, we choose always to be shepherdesses, and for our main occupation to be watching over our flocks, because we believe that a long experience of the solitary life will make us gain what you possess naturally—it will give us wit and insight, will raise our souls to the contemplation of heavenly things, and will make us worthy of being governed by the greatest princess in the world. Our earliest ancestors, who were themselves great princes, did not scorn this occupation, and the care of their flocks did not keep them from reaching as far as the heavens and becoming the first to ponder the different effects of the stars. That is why we will value the honor of being like them and of enriching our simplicity with the greatest treasures in life. We want only small huts where magnificence will be forbidden, and where we will allow only what is necessary. Each one of us will choose the site of their residence according to their own inclination, and while you prefer a view to the other beauties of the countryside, I would wish, for my own, the darkness of the forest, where I would hope that nature would display some of the beauties that you describe and that streams and meadows

---

6. "The shepherds of Lignon" are characters in Honoré d'Urfé's novel *L'Astrée.*

où je voudrais que la nature fît trouver quelques-unes des beautés dont vous faites la description et que les eaux et les prés aussi bien que la forêt se rencontrassent auprès de mon habitation, les autres en useraient de même, car la liberté gouvernée par la raison et la justice ferait un de nos plus sensibles plaisirs. Je voudrais que dans toutes ces petites maisons il y eût des chambres lambrissées de bois tout uni dont le seul ornement serait la netteté, et que chacun de nous eût un cabinet qui selon vos ordres, belle Amelinte, fut rempli de bons livres[.] Les hommes savants y produiraient des ouvrages dignes d'éterniser notre champêtre République, et nous autres Bergères nous apprendrions en lisant à perfectionner notre vie et nos mœurs et à jouir de ce repos que nous aurions préféré aux turbulentes agitations de la Cour et du monde. Je voudrais que par vos lois il nous fût permis de n'avoir que deux personnes pour nous servir, car on a toujours remarqué que la quantité de valets trouble le calme des familles. Ce nombre suffirait pour nous apprêter les choses nécessaires au soutien de la vie, et au soin de la netteté, et pour garder nos troupeaux quand les saisons fâcheuses nous empêcheraient de nous y occuper nous-mêmes avec plaisir. Nos habits, Grande Princesse, seraient simples mais propres, et je crois que vous approuveriez qu'ils fussent aussi éloignés de la vanité que de la laideur, car il me semble qu'il est nécessaire pour la société civile de se plaire les uns aux autres, et pourvu que cet agrément ne passe point des yeux dans le cœur, vous auriez sujet d'être satisfaite de la sagesse de vos sujets: c'est avec raison, Illustre Princesse, que vous avez banni la galanterie de leur commerce pour y établir seulement le plaisir de la conversation, qui assurément est le seul estimable parmi les honnêtes gens; mais j'ai grand-peur que cette loi si sage et si nécessaire ne fût mal observée, et comme en ce cas vous seriez contrainte d'y apporter du remède. Je pense qu'enfin vous vous trouveriez obligée de permettre parmi nous cette vieille et légitime coutume qui s'appelle mariage. Il est fâcheux d'être malade et plus encore de prendre médecine pour se guérir, mais comme les hommes les plus sains sont ceux qui sont les moins malades, et que les plus parfaits sont ceux seulement qui tendent le plus à la perfection, de même ceux de vos bergers qui approcheraient le plus de celle que vous leur inspireriez par votre exemple, et que vous leur commandez par vos ordonnances seraient les plus louables, vous estimeriez ceux-là, vous pardonneriez aux autres et vous tireriez cet avantage de leur imperfection que vos Lois et votre République par leur durée rendraient votre gloire immortelle. La politesse que vous introduisez parmi vos solitaires sujets me fait craindre qu'ils n'aient l'esprit galant, il est même assez raisonnable aux jeunes gens d'aimer les vers, et même d'en faire, il serait assez difficile cela étant d'empêcher que les bergères ne les écoutassent, et j'aurais peur que leurs fictions ne leur parussent trop véritables. Il faut savoir

as well as woods could be found near my house. The others would make similar choices, for a liberty governed by reason and justice would be one of our greatest pleasures. I would like there to be, in all of these little houses, rooms paneled with wood whose only ornament would be symmetry, and that each of us would have a study,[7] which, according to your orders, beautiful Amelinte, would be filled with good books. There, learned men would produce works worthy of immortalizing our rural Republic, and we shepherdesses would learn through reading how to perfect our life and our morals and to enjoy the repose that we would prefer to the turbulent agitation of the court and society. I would like your laws to allow us to have only two people to serve us, for it has always been said that a large number of valets disrupts a family's peacefulness. This number would be enough to prepare our daily necessities, to keep things clean, and to watch over our flocks when the inclement seasons would keep us from doing this ourselves with pleasure. Our clothing, great Princess, would be simple yet neat, and I believe that you would consent to it being as removed from vanity as from ugliness, for it seems to me that in civilized society each member must please the others, and so long as this charm does not travel from the eyes to the heart, you would have reason to be satisfied with your subjects' good sense. You were right, illustrious Princess, to have banished gallantry[8] from our commerce in order to favor solely the pleasure of conversation, which is surely the only respectable one for people of quality; but I fear that this very wise and necessary law will be but poorly observed, and since in such a case you must supply a remedy, I think that in the end you will be forced to allow the time-honored and legitimate custom called marriage. It is annoying to be sick and even more so to have to take medicine in order to get well, but since the healthiest men are the ones who are the least sick, and the best ones are only those who tend the most toward perfection, similarly those among your shepherds who would come closest to the perfection that your example would inspire in them and to which your laws would compel them would be the most praiseworthy, you would respect them, you would forgive the others, and the advantage that you would gain from their imperfection is that,

7. The French "cabinet" in this case refers to a small, private room reserved for intellectual pursuits.

8. The French "galanterie" and its adjective "galant" often appear in this correspondence. They have a range of meanings from the English "gallant" to "noble," "chivalrous," or "charming." The phrase "un galant" can refer to a man of the court or a gentleman. "Galanterie" is a particularly tricky term. Whereas at times it can share the positive connotations of the English "gallantry," it can also mean flirtation, or even seduction. In those instances Montpensier obviously considers "galanterie" a dangerous game and a threat to the stability of her community.

connaître le péril pour l'éviter, mais toutes n'auront pas peut-être assez de prudence pour se sauver par les belles voies, c'est pourquoi il est à propos de leur en donner de celles, qui du moins si elles sont privées de gloire ne le sont pas d'innocence, car je souhaite qu'elles soient sages par leur choix et qu'elles fuient plutôt par inclination que par la défense que vous leur en feriez. Les plus belles apprendront en vous voyant qu'on peut être belle, spirituelle et sage tout ensemble; par vos sages préceptes, vertueuse Amelinte, vous leur persuaderez que les grâces que nous recevons du ciel ne nous doivent pas convier à l'offenser, et qu'elles seraient bien méprisables d'en faire un mauvais usage dans les déserts, puisque vous, Grande Princesse, avez conservé tous ces avantages dans toute leur pureté au milieu de la cour, dans la Royale maison des Rois vos Aïeux où vous avez eu sans doute des Esclaves que vous avez méprisés, où l'on vous a donné des louanges sans que vous ayez daigné les écouter, et où vous avez été l'admiration des hommes et des femmes et celle de toute l'Europe qui est partout remplie de l'éclat de votre gloire[.]

LETTRE 3

Mademoiselle
à Madame de Motteville

Je m'aperçois par votre réponse que vous n'avez qu'à oser, que vous pouvez tout ce qui vous plaît et que j'ai eu tort d'en être en doute, mais je suis dans un extrême étonnement lorsque vous me voulez prouver par de vives raisons qu'il est non seulement à propos, mais aussi nécessaire de se marier. Pour moi je ne le comprends point, cependant comme il faut avoir beaucoup de connaissance des choses pour en parler pertinemment, comme il faudrait vous dire de bonnes raisons pour détruire les vôtres et que c'en serait une fort mauvaise de vous dire que ce n'est pas mon avis, je me servirai en cela de

because of their longevity, your laws and your Republic would make your glory immortal. The politeness that you introduce among your isolated subjects makes me fear that the spirit of gallantry will also be present. It is even somewhat to be expected that young men will like poetry and will even write it: this being the case, it would be rather difficult to keep the shepherdesses from listening to them, and I am afraid that their fictions will appear only too truthful to them. One must know how to recognize danger if it is to be avoided, but perhaps not everyone will have enough prudence to take the right path to save themselves. This is why it is opportune to indicate to them the ways that even if they are devoid of glory, at least will not be devoid of innocence, for I hope that they will be wise by their own choice and that they will run from [gallantry] because of their own inclination rather than because of the rules that you had imposed. The most beautiful [among them] will learn by seeing you that it is possible to be beautiful, witty, and sensible all at the same time. Through your wise precepts, virtuous Amelinte, you will persuade them that the charms that heaven bestows upon us should not encourage us to offend it, and that they would make themselves contemptible if they put their charms to bad use in our wilderness, since you, noble Princess, have maintained these advantages in all their purity in the midst of the court, in the royal house of the kings, your ancestors, where you have certainly always had slaves that you have scorned, where you were given praise without having ever deigned to listen to it, and where you have been admired by men and women and by all Europe, which is everywhere filled with the brilliance of your glory.

LETTER 3

Mademoiselle
to Madame de Motteville

I see by your response that you have only to dare, that you can do anything that you like, and that I was wrong to doubt this. I am extremely surprised, however, that you want to prove to me with perceptive reasons that it is not only appropriate, but also necessary to get married. For my part, I don't understand your reasoning at all; nevertheless, since it is necessary to know things well in order to talk about them judiciously, since it is necessary to give good reasons to defeat yours, and since it is very inadequate simply to say that it is not my own view, in this matter I will put to use the authority

cette autorité que me donne le sang de tous les Rois dont vous dites que je suis descendue, je vous maintiendrai avec assurance qu'il me semble que l'on doit déférer à mon sentiment, que mon avis doit être le maître des autres. Enfin ce que disaient mes Pères, que tel est mon plaisir, et tant pis pour ceux qui n'y trouveraient pas le leur. Néanmoins pour faire voir que je n'agis pas si absolument je tâcherai de vous faire connaître que ce n'est point une chose sans exemple que de voir les personnes accommoder leurs inclinations au goût et à l'humeur de ceux de qui on dépend. La Marquise de Senecé m'a dit que dans le village de Randan en Auvergne jamais une veuve ne s'est remariée et n'en avait témoigné la moindre envie à quelque âge qu'elle eût perdu son mari, par ce que feu la Comtesse de Randan en a usé ainsi, et apparemment la Marquise de Senecé et la Comtesse de Fleix ne feront pas changer cette bonne coutume.[5] Par là vous pouvez connaître le pouvoir de bons exemples et combien il prévaut sur les méchantes coutumes, et n'aurais-je pas lieu de croire que l'autorité du mien pourrait détruire dans nos déserts cette erreur qui s'est tournée en bienséance[?] Mon Empire se bornerait là, c'est pourquoi personne n'aurait droit de murmurer contre moi-même, j'étendrais ma bonté jusqu'à permettre que ceux qui auraient envie de se marier nous quittassent plutôt que de rendre notre solitude une habitation de gens sujets aux imperfections de la nature, tout le monde n'a pas la force de la surmonter, et Monsieur de Luynes nous apprend que la grâce n'en est pas toujours la maîtresse.[6]

Peut-être conviendrez-vous qu'il est plus aisé de ne pas se remarier que de ne s'être jamais mariée, et je demeurerai d'accord que cela peut être, mais rien ne me persuade qu'on puisse avoir envie de se marier quand on est guéri de l'ambition. Or dans notre désert on y renonce absolument, et à toute sorte d'intérêt. Il n'y a donc que l'amour seul qui puisse inspirer cette fantaisie, et c'est pour cela qu'il me semble que je n'avais pas mal fait de le bannir d'entre nous. Vous voulez qu'il y demeure, ou plutôt vous craigniez qu'il ne soit

5. Marie-Catherine de La Rochefoucauld (1588–1677) married Henri de Bauffremont, baron de Senecé (also written "Senecey" and "Sennecy") in 1607. He died in 1622 of wounds received at the siege of Royan. She never remarried. After her husband's death, she became first a lady-in-waiting to Anne of Austria and then the governess of Louis XIV. Her daughter, Marie-Claire de Bauffremont-Senecé (d. 1680), married Jean-Baptiste de Foix de Candale, comte de Fleix, in 1637, was widowed in 1646, and never remarried. The comté of Randan had been associated with the La Rochefoucauld family since the early sixteenth century. The title count of Randan was transmitted through the female line. Randan was made a duchy in 1661 to thank the marquise de Senecé for her services to the Crown; the royal charter specified that the title would be passed on to her daughter. Today Randan is a village in Auvergne.

6. Louis-Charles d'Albert, duc de Luynes (1620–1690): prolific author of works on religion and personal morality; translator of the Bible and of Descartes's meditations. From a very early age, he chose to live in seclusion from the court.

given to me by the blood of all the kings from which you say I descend: I will maintain with confidence that I think everyone should defer to my conviction, that my opinion should prevail. Lastly, as my fathers used to say, such is my pleasure and too bad for those who do not find it to be theirs. Nonetheless, to show that I do not act so absolutely, I will try to prove to you that it is not unprecedented to see people adapt their inclination to the taste and humor of those on whom they depend. The marquise de Senecé told me that in the town of Randan in Auvergne no widow ever remarried, nor even showed the slightest desire to do so, no matter what her age when she lost her husband, because the late comtesse de Randan had not done so, and apparently the marquise de Senecé and the comtesse de Fleix will not have this good custom changed.[9] From this, you can see the power of good examples and how they prevail over bad customs, and judge if I have reason to believe that the authority of my example could, in our wilderness, destroy this error that has become accepted as correct behavior. My empire would stop there; that is why no one would have the right to complain about me. I would extend my goodness even so far as to allow those who want to marry to leave us rather than to make our solitude a haven for people subject to the imperfections of nature; not everyone is strong enough to resist marriage, and Monsieur de Luynes teaches us that grace is not always able to master it.[10]

Perhaps you will argue that it is easier not to remarry than never to marry at all, and I will agree that that may be, but nothing will persuade me that anyone can desire to be married once they have been cured of that ambition. Thus, in our wilderness everyone would renounce ambition completely, along with all self-interest. In that case, only love could inspire this whim, and that is why I think that I have not been wrong to banish it from among us. You want it to remain, or rather, you fear that we must allow it, but must

9. Marie-Catherine de La Rochefoucauld (1588–1677) married Henri de Bauffremont, baron de Senecé (also written "Senecey" and "Sennecy") in 1607. He died in 1622 of wounds received at the siege of Royan. She never remarried. After her husband's death, she became first a lady-in-waiting to Anne of Austria and then the governess of Louis XIV. Her daughter, Marie-Claire de Bauffremont-Senecé (d. 1680), married Jean-Baptiste de Foix de Candale, comte de Fleix, in 1637, was widowed in 1646, and never remarried. The comté of Randan had been associated with the La Rochefoucauld family since the early sixteenth century. The title count of Randan was transmitted through the female line. Randan was made a duchy in 1661 to thank the marquise de Senecé for her services to the Crown; the royal charter specified that the title would be passed on to her daughter. Today Randan is a village in Auvergne.

10. Louis-Charles d'Albert, duc de Luynes (1620–1690): prolific author of works on religion and personal morality; translator of the Bible and of Descartes's meditations. From a very early age, he chose to live in seclusion from the court.

nécessaire de le permettre, mais y dois-je consentir? Songez que de l'amitié on va souvent à l'amour, et n'avez-vous point aussi pensé quelquefois à ces vers.

C'est un penchant si doux qu'on y tombe sans peine
Mais quand il faut changer l'amour en amitié
Que l'âme qui s'y force est digne de pitié!

Je serais d'avis que dans toutes les maisons ces vers fussent écrits en quelque endroit remarquable comme une sentence infaillible, parce qu'assurément on en pourrait profiter; mais comme rien ne nous lie et ne nous contraint dans notre société nous nous garantirons encore du mariage par cette liberté que nous nous conserverions. Elle serait plutôt un frein pour les passions qu'une obligation contraignante, au lieu que dès qu'on est obligé à quelque chose on la hait, on la déteste et on voudrait en être dehors. Cette chère liberté nous ferait connaître qu'il suffit de pouvoir les choses pour ne les pas vouloir. La raison et le bon sens seraient notre seul vœu et nos seules obligations. On considérerait ce penchant et sa douceur pour plaindre ceux qui s'y laisse-raient tomber et pour n'y pas glisser soi-même, on remarquerait que le retour en est fâcheux, et quelle pitié est-ce de revenir de l'amour à l'amitié, l'une est honnête commode et nécessaire au commerce de la vie et à sa douceur. Ce bon sens et cette raison dont je fais tant de cas y portent tout à fait; c'est un plaisir de durée de toutes sortes de personnes, d'âge et de condition, com-mandé[7] même par les Lois divines. L'autre au contraire est défendu, son com-merce est honteux, il est volage et inégal, sans foi et sans probité, c'est un Enfant sans raison et qui ne la connaît point. Il ne cause que des inquiétudes, des embarras et des jalousies. Si on pense l'avoir arrêté il échappe, et les pleurs et les gémissemens ne le font point revenir: enfin sous quelque prétexte que ce soit il ne me semble nullement propre à demeurer avec nous, car c'est un impie, il se moque du sacrement, il n'en use que comme ces Turcs qui sont aux Galères lesquels pour quitter leurs chaînes se font baptiser et puis s'en retournent en leur pays plus Turcs que jamais. Voilà comme il fait, vous y fieriez-vous après cela, et voudriez-vous avoir des Renégats parmi nous? Tout de bon cela serait terrible et encore plus que ce soit vous qui l'ayez pro-posé, j'en suis honteuse pour vous, mais je vois bien à quoi il en faudra venir pour éviter le mariage, il faut expliquer la galanterie dont vous avez tant de peur, car de soi c'est une chose honnête bien que souvent on la prenne en mauvaise part dans le monde et qu'on la tourne du mauvais côté comme l'on

---

7. This is the only place where I had to modify the French text in a significant manner: the manuscript reads "d'âge, et de condition commandées."

I consent? Consider that from friendship, one often falls into love, and have you not also sometimes thought of these verses:

> It is an inclination so sweet that one succumbs to it
> But when love must be changed into amity
> How the soul that constrains itself is worthy of pity!

It is my opinion that these verses should be inscribed as an infallible maxim in a conspicuous place in every house, because everyone can surely profit from them. Since in our society nothing binds and constrains us, the liberty that we would preserve for ourselves will protect us against marriage. It would be more of a check for our passions than a restricting obligation: when we are forced to do something, it becomes hateful, detestable, and we want to be free of it. This precious liberty would show us that it is enough to be able to do something not to want to do it. Our only vows and obligations would be to reason and good sense. We would remember this penchant [for marriage] and its sweetness and pity those who let themselves succumb to it, and to avoid being drawn in ourselves, we would remind ourselves that the way back is painful, and what a shame it is to return from love to friendship. The latter is reasonable, comfortable, and necessary to the commerce of life and to its sweetness. The good sense and reason that are so important to me lead to it; it is a long-lived pleasure befitting all sorts of people, of all ages and conditions, one that even divine law commands. The other, on the contrary, is forbidden; its commerce is shameful. It is flighty and inconsistent, without faith or integrity; it is presided over by an unreasonable child who has never experienced love. It causes only worry, trouble, and jealousy. If you think you have caught it, it escapes, and tears and moans will not make it return. Finally, I do not think it at all suited to lodge with us under any pretext, for it is impious: it mocks the sacrament and treats it like those Turks in the galleys who, in order to escape from their chains, have themselves baptized and then return to their country more Turkish than ever. That is how it acts; would you trust it after that, and would you have renegades among us? Truly, it would be terrible and even more so because it would have been because of your suggestion. I am really sorry about this for your sake, but I see clearly the lengths to which we must go to avoid marriage. We must come to understand gallantry, the thing you fear so much, for in itself it is an honorable thing, even though it is often misunderstood by those at court,[11] who take a dim view of it, as can always happen if one has bad intentions. That noble

---

11. The phrase "le monde," literally, "the world," designated those who frequented the court.

peut faire toutes choses lorsqu'on est mal intentionné. Cette belle galanterie qui se peut souffrir parmi nous est assurément bienséante, l'air galant peut convenir à tout et puisque l'on a souvent dit que Sainte Thérèse avait l'esprit galant, qui ne le voudrait point avoir? Puisqu'on voyait le même air dans tout ce que faisait l'Infante Isabelle, qui ne voudrait pas que sa manière d'agir imitât la sienne? Enfin cette galanterie générale et sans objet est ce qui se peut permettre parmi nous. Je conviens qu'on la peut rechercher dans nos habits avec cette propreté et modestie que vous y désireriez et qui sont aussi fort à mon gré, même je souffrirais que cet ajustement se pût louer comme la bonne santé qui paraîtrait sur le visage, cela n'étant dit que quand il serait vrai ne me paraîtrait point une cajolerie, et les louanges véritables se peuvent donner par un esprit de cordialité et d'amitié que j'aimerais fort, aussi bien que les soins et la complaisance qu'on aurait les uns pour les autres; toutefois je m'en dispense moi-même par ce que ce n'est pas mon esprit, peut-être aussi n'en serais-je pas incapable, parce que sans que je m'en aperçoive la bonté de mon naturel souvent me fait faire des choses que je ne ferais pas si j'y songeais, car je crois n'être pas complaisante naturellement. Je voudrais que les hommes eussent pour les Dames ces déférences que les honnêtes gens doivent avoir, et qu'ils fussent toujours devant elles dans un esprit d'honnêteté et de galanterie, ce que ne font point ceux qu'on appelle les galants du temps, car ils n'ont nulle civilité pour les femmes. Je ne voudrais pas qu'ils en usassent tout à fait comme ces galants qui sont décrits dans les Romans, mais j'en voudrais quelque chose. Je prendrais de tout un peu pour perfectionner nos habitants de l'un et de l'autre sexe, mais comme rien n'a été parfait en ce monde il me serait aussi difficile d'exprimer ce qui est nécessaire pour cela. J'ajouterai seulement, et vous en conviendrez sans doute avec moi, qu'il serait bon que toutes nos Dames eussent une conduite nette et sans reproche, et contre qui la calomnie n'eût pu faire d'impression; car pour n'avoir jamais connu sa malice, c'est une chose presque impossible, les hommes qui blasphèment sans cesse contre le Créateur peuvent bien blasphémer contre ses créatures. Je souhaiterais par la même raison que ceux qui seraient de profession à porter l'épée fussent braves et qu'ils eussent acquis de la gloire dans leur métier, que nos Docteurs eussent une science extraordinaire et que leurs mœurs fussent capables de servir d'exemple, et ainsi de tous les autres; mais pour conclure par où j'ai commencé vous souffrirez encore que je vous dise que ce qui a donné la supériorité aux hommes a été le mariage, et que ce qui nous a fait nommer le sexe fragile a été cette dépendance où l'usage nous a assujetties souvent contre notre volonté et par des raisons de famille dont nous avons été les victimes. Enfin tirons-nous de l'esclavage, qu'il y ait un coin du monde où l'on

sort of gallantry, which can be allowed among us, is certainly seemly; a gallant manner is always appropriate, and since it has often been said that Saint Teresa herself had one, who would not want to be like her? Since the same manner was evident in everything that the Infanta Isabella did, who would not want to imitate her behavior? In short: the kind of gallantry that is nonspecific and without a particular object can be tolerated among us. I agree that we should strive for it in our clothing with the neatness and modesty that you desire and that are also very much to my liking. I would even tolerate this small concession being praised like the good health that is apparent just by looking at someone's face. If we only say this when it is true, it would not seem to me to be flattery at all, and such truthful compliments can be given in a spirit of cordiality and friendliness that would please me very much, as would the care and kindness that we would all show each other. Nevertheless, I will excuse myself from it because it is not in my character. Perhaps though I would not be incapable of it since, without even realizing it, the kindness of my nature often makes me do things that I would not do if I stopped to think about them, for I do not believe myself to be naturally obliging. I would hope that the men would display that deference that people of quality should show toward women and that, in their presence, they would always behave in the spirit of courtesy and gallantry, which the so-called gentlemen of this era do not at all demonstrate, since they show no civility toward women. I would not want them to act exactly like the heroes who are depicted in novels, though I would like something of this manner. I would take a little from many sources in order to perfect the members of our community of both sexes, but since nothing in this world has ever been perfect, it would be difficult for me to convey what would be necessary for the task. I will only add, and you will doubtless agree with me, that it would be good for all our ladies to conduct themselves in a strict and irreproachable manner, in order that they not be subject to calumny. Never to have known its malice is almost impossible: men who constantly utter blasphemies against the creator can easily do the same against his creatures. I would hope, for the same reason, that those who bear a sword [12] would be brave and that they would have gained glory in the army, that our theologians would be extraordinarily knowledgeable and that their conduct, and indeed that of all the others, would be exemplary. And, to finish where I began, you will allow me to tell you again that marriage is that which has given men the

---

12. In France only the highest nobility had the right to wear a sword.

puisse dire que les femmes sont maîtresses d'elles-mêmes, et qu'elles n'ont pas tous les défauts qu'on leur attribue et célébrons-nous dans les siècles à venir par une vie qui nous fasse vivre éternellement.

LETTRE 4

Madame de Motteville
à Mademoiselle

Il est difficile que je puisse trouver des raisons pour combattre vos sentiments, et j'ose dire que les miens ont quelque rapport à vos maximes, je n'ai été soumise à ce lien qui vous déplaît si fort que deux seules années de ma vie, quand la liberté me fut rendue j'étais dans cet âge qui semblait me convier à suivre les honnêtes faiblesses des humains, mais cette liberté m'a toujours semblé préférable à tous les autres biens que l'on estime dans le monde, et de la manière que j'en ai usé il semble que j'aie été habitante du village de Randan. Ces Illustres veuves Madame la Marquise de Senecé et Madame la Comtesse de Fleix sa fille qui se sont signalées par mille belles qualités qu'elles possèdent, et par la gloire de leur veuvage sont des Dames dont j'ai toujours estimé la conduite. Je vois toujours avec joie que la chasteté a fait de grands saints, j'envie même aux Païens l'honneur qu'ils ont eu d'avoir eu des Vestales parmi eux, elles ont mérité par leur pureté que Dieu qui parmi toutes sortes de nations est toujours le protecteur de la verité et de l'innocence ait fait des merveilles en leur faveur, c'est pourquoi, Grande Princesse, je suis beaucoup plus disposée à vous admirer qu'à vous contredire, et à vous obéir qu'à vous résister. Vous décrivez d'une manière admirable les défauts de ce petit Tyran qui cause tant de maux aux hommes, il suffit de votre haine pour le faire rejeter de tous ceux qui jusqu'à présent l'ont révéré et qui souvent l'ont suivi malgré eux. Vous ressemblez à ces grands capitaines qui sont accoutumés à vaincre: dès aussitôt que vous l'avez voulu combattre vous l'avez taillé en pièces, après l'avoir défait vous l'avez envoyé aux galères, et n'étant pas résolue de le bien traiter en aucune condition vous ne l'en avez tiré qu'à sa honte; mes armes sont trop faibles pour espérer de lui pouvoir faire du mal après vous, mais comme grâces au ciel je le méprise autant qu'il le mérite souffrez je vous

upper hand, that this dependence to which custom subjects us, often against our will and because of family obligations of which we have been the victims, is what has caused us to be named the weaker sex. Let us at last deliver ourselves from this slavery; let there be a corner of the world in which it can be said that women are their own mistresses and do not have all the faults that are attributed to them; and let us celebrate ourselves for the centuries to come through a way of life that will immortalize us.

LETTER 4

Madame de Motteville

to Mademoiselle

It is hard for me to find reasons to combat your sentiments, and I dare say that mine have some relation to your maxims. I was subjected to this bond that so displeases you for only two years of my life; when my freedom was restored to me, I was at an age that seemed to invite me to imitate honorable human weaknesses. However, liberty always seemed preferable to me to all the other possessions valued by those of our station, and because of the manner in which I exercised mine, one would think that I had been a resident of the town of Randan. Those illustrious widows, Madame la marquise de Senecé and her daughter Madame la comtesse de Fleix, who have distinguished themselves by the many fine qualities they possess and because of the glory of their widowhood, are ladies whose conduct I have always respected. I always note with joy that chastity has produced great saints. I even envy the pagans the honor of having had vestals among them, whose purity inspired God—always the protector of truth and innocence in all places—to work miracles. This is why, great Princess, I am much more inclined to admire you than to contradict you, and to obey you rather than to resist you. You describe, in an admirable way, the faults of this petty tyrant who causes so much harm to mankind: your hatred is enough to cause those to dismiss him who have until now worshiped him and followed him in spite of themselves. You are like those great captains who are used to victory; as soon as you decided to fight him, you cut him to pieces; after having defeated him, you sent him to the galleys; and, resolved not to treat him well under any circumstances, you have only brought him back in order to shame him. My weapons are too weak to hope to do him any additional harm, but since, thanks to the mercy of heaven, I despise him as much as he deserves, I beg you,

supplie, Illustre Princesse, que je sois un des Soldats de votre armée, que je puisse du moins m'enrôler au nombre de ses Ennemis, que je lui porte quelque coup, et que je puisse tout abattu qu'il est à vos pieds lui dire encore quelques injures, il est toujours à craindre que n'osant se défendre contre vous par le respect qu'il vous porte il ne puisse à la derobée tirer encore des flèches par le monde, et peut-être que vos bergères malgré toutes vos précautions en pourraient avoir leur part; c'est pourquoi il n'y a pas de danger que petits et grands lui courrent sus,[8] on ne saurait trop le diffamer pour les mauvais tours qu'il a faits au genre humain, et la tyrannie qu'il exerce sur notre sexe nous doit obliger à l'outrager en toutes les occasions où nous pourrons nous venger de lui. Les hommes par lui sont nos plus cruels Ennemis; quand les Dames les aiment c'est alors qu'ils prétendent avoir plus de droit de les persécuter, et les faveurs qu'elles leur font se tournent d'ordinaire pour elles en de célèbres mais honteuses aventures. Ils cachent sous ces beaux mots d'adoration, de respect, et de passion les armes dont ils offensent la gloire de celles qu'ils paraissent estimer, et qu'ils méprisent en effet[.] Elles souffrent par leurs trahisons de violentes douleurs, et l'amour légitime par la froideur de son poison les prive souvent de bonheur, ceux même de quelque sexe qu'ils soient qui sont assez fols pour croire que ces peines sont préférables aux autres plaisirs nous avoueront

> Que el mas feliz Estado
> En que pone El Amor al que bien ama
> En fin trae un cuidado.[9]

Je sais toutes ces vérités, Belle Amelinte, je sais de plus que les Lois qui nous soumettent à leur puissance sont dures et insupportables, je sais qu'ils les ont faites injustes à notre égard et trop avantageuses pour eux, ils usurpent sur nous le commandement de la mer et de la terre, les sciences, la valeur, la puissance, celle de juger et d'être les maîtres de la vie des humains, les dignités en toutes conditions, et[,] ôté la quenouille, je ne sais rien sous le Soleil qu'ils n'aient mis de leur côté; cependant leur tyrannie n'est fondée sur aucun juste prétexte. Les histoires sont pleines de femmes qui ont gouverné des Empires avec une singulière prudence, qui ont acquis de la gloire en commandant des armées et qui se sont fait admirer par leur capacité[.] La politique n'a point de secrets qu'Isabelle de Castille, Elizabeth d'Angleterre, la Duchesse de Parme et Catherine de Médicis dans nos derniers siècles n'aient sus

---

8. "Courrent sus": a hunting term, signifying to be in hot pursuit.

9. Motteville was fluent enough in Spanish to have served as interpreter for Montpensier during the wedding festivities.

illustrious Princess, to allow me to be one of the soldiers in your army, so that I can at least enlist myself in the ranks of his enemies, that I can inflict a small blow, and that, vanquished as he is at your feet, I can humiliate him even further. It is still to be feared that, not being able to defend himself against you because of the respect he bears you, he would nonetheless be able surreptitiously to shoot his arrows the world over, and perhaps, in spite of all your precautions, your shepherdesses might be wounded by them. This is why there is no danger in both great and small trying to pursue him hotly. We can never cease vilifying him on account of the cruel tricks he has played on the human race, and the tyranny that he exerts over our sex forces us to disparage him whenever we have the opportunity to avenge ourselves. Thanks to him, men are our most cruel enemies: when ladies love them, they then claim to have even more right to persecute them, and the favors that women bestow on men usually result in adventures that, while celebrated, bring only shame to our sex. Under their lovely words of adoration, respect, and passion, men hide the weapons they use to insult the honor of those whom they seem to respect, and whom they actually despise. Women endure great suffering because of these betrayals, and legitimate love, because its poison is so cold, often deprives them of happiness. Those, of either sex, who are foolish enough to believe that these pains are preferable to other pleasures will confess to us

> That the most happy State
> In which Love puts the one who loves well
> In the end brings care.[13]

I know all these truths, beautiful Amelinte; furthermore, I know that the laws that subject us to their power are hard and unbearable; I know that men have made them unfair for us and too advantageous for themselves. They take away from us dominion over the sea and the earth, the sciences, merit, power—that of judging and being the master of human lives—and dignity in all situations, and, with the exception of the distaff, I know of nothing under the sun that they have not appropriated; even though their tyranny has no just basis. The history books are full of women who have governed empires with singular wisdom, who have gained glory by commanding armies, and whose abilities have given rise to great admiration; in recent centuries, there were no secrets in politics that Isabella of Castile, Elizabeth of England, the duchess of Parma, and Catherine de Médicis did not know and practice; and we

---

13. These lines are in Spanish in the French original. Motteville was fluent enough in Spanish to have served as interpreter for Montpensier during the wedding festivities.

et pratiqués, et dans le nôtre nous avons vu que les sciences qui malgré les hommes se sont rendues familières en tous les temps à beaucoup de femmes ont enrichi l'esprit de la princesse Elisabeth de Bohème de Mademoiselle de Schurman en Hollande, de Madame de Brassac et de Mademoiselle de Scudéry en France.[10] Les histoires célèbrent les louanges de beaucoup d'autres, et leur savoir ne leur a point ôté leur modestie et la douceur convenable à notre sexe. La chasteté est en nous une vertu nécessaire, sans elle toutes les autres perdent leur lustre, c'est pourquoi il est injuste de nous borner à celle-là. Je pense même qu'ils ne nous l'auraient pas donnée en partage sans qu'ils [aient][11] pensé que comme elle nous doit être facile à pratiquer ils prétendent aussi que nous en méritons peu de gloire. J'en demeure d'accord et je suis persuadée que ce serait pour nous une chose aisée de nous délivrer de cet esclavage par la liberté de notre cœur et la pureté de nos sentiments. Car je ne doute pas que beaucoup de Dames d'elles-mêmes ne soient capables de cette perfection, mais, Grande Princesse, vous voulez des hommes dans votre Etat et vous ne voulez pas vous souvenir que leur corruption se pourra communiquer à celles de notre sexe qui ne seront pas aussi fortes que vous, c'est pourquoi j'avais cru qu'il était de votre prudence d'obvier aux inconvenients qui pourraient arriver parmi vos sujets, leur vertu ne peut pas être égale en tous, car il n'y a rien de si naturel à l'homme que le défaut et le changement. Malgré les vertus que j'attribue à notre sexe il faut avouer qu'en général la vanité et l'amour-propre sont les ordinaires défauts des Dames, et que l'oisiveté quasi inévitable où les hommes les ont exposées en les jugeant incapables des grandes choses les porte trop ardemment à désirer d'acquérir de la gloire par leur beauté et par les louanges qu'elles en attendent. Je ne doute pas que votre seul exemple ne couvrît leur engagement de honte et que la liberté ne leur parût plus estimable qu'un fâcheux esclavage, c'est assez l'ordinaire des peuples de haïr ce que les Souverains ne pratiquent pas, et ce qui se fait à l'égard des mauvaises coutumes se doit beaucoup plutôt espérer en faveur des

---

10. Elizabeth of Bohemia (1618–1680): student of Descartes, who publicly professed his admiration for her abilities. She incurred her parents' anger when she steadfastly refused a series of prestigious marriages they had arranged for her in order to devote herself to intellectual pursuits.

   Anna Maria van Schurman (1607–1678): painter, linguist, poet, author of many publications in Latin, correspondent of the most learned men of the day, famous all over Europe for her erudition; she refused to marry. Cf. Anna Maria van Schurman, *Whether a Christian Woman Should Be Educated and Other Writings from Her Intellectual Circle.* Ed. and trans. Joyce L. Irwin (Chicago: University of Chicago Press, 1998).

   Catherine de Sainte-Maure, comtesse de Brassac (d. 1648): lady-in-waiting to Anne of Austria; she had a celebrated collection of portraits of the French royal family.

   Madeleine de Scudéry (1607–1701): highly prolific author and the most celebrated French novelist of the first half of the seventeenth century; she never married.

11. The manuscript reads "ont."

have seen that the sciences, practiced in every age by many women, in spite
of the opposition of men, have, in our own day, enriched the minds of
Elizabeth of Bohemia, Mademoiselle van Schurman in Holland, Madame de
Brassac and Mademoiselle de Scudéry in France.[14] History sings the praise
of many other women whose knowledge did not take away their modesty
and the gentleness that befits our sex. Chastity is for us a necessary virtue;
without it all the others lose their luster: that is why it is unfair to limit us to
this virtue alone. I do not even think that we would have been endowed with
it, if men did not think that since it is easy for us to follow, they could therefore claim that we deserve little glory for it. I agree and I am convinced that
it would be an easy thing for us to liberate ourselves from this slavery because of the freedom of our hearts and the purity of our feelings. I have no
doubt that many ladies are capable of this perfection. You, noble Princess,
however, want men in your state and you do not want to remember that their
corruption could be communicated to those of our sex who are not as strong
as you. This is why I thought that in your wisdom you would take precautions
to avoid any difficulties that could arise among your subjects: all of them
cannot be equally virtuous, for there is nothing more natural to mankind than
moral frailty and inconsistency. In spite of the virtues that I attribute to our
sex, I must admit that, in general, vanity and pride are women's most common faults, and that the almost inevitable idleness into which they have been
forced by the men who deem them incapable of great things leads them too
ardently to desire glory through their beauty and the praises that they expect because of it. I do not doubt that your example alone would make them
ashamed of this desire and that liberty would seem more valuable than a de-
plorable slavery. Their subjects usually despise what their sovereigns do not
practice: since this is the case with ill-advised customs, we might rather hope
that it will also be true of admirable ones. If by some misfortune the less perfect fall in love, however, they[15] could at least quote Saint Paul's maxims to

14. Elizabeth of Bohemia (1618–1680): student of Descartes, who publicly professed his admiration for her abilities. She incurred her parents' anger when she steadfastly refused a series of
prestigious marriages they had arranged for her in order to devote herself to intellectual pursuits.

   Anna Maria van Schurman (1607–1678): painter, linguist, poet, author of many publications in Latin, correspondent of the most learned men of the day, famous all over Europe for
her erudition; she refused to marry. Cf. Anna Maria van Schurman, *Whether a Christian Woman
Should Be Educated and Other Writings from Her Intellectual Circle*. Ed. and trans. Joyce L. Irwin (Chicago: University of Chicago Press, 1998).

   Catherine de Sainte-Maure, comtesse de Brassac (d. 1648): lady-in-waiting to Anne of
Austria; she had a celebrated collection of portraits of the French royal family.

   Madeleine de Scudéry (1607–1701): highly prolific author and the most celebrated French
novelist of the first half of the seventeenth century; she never married.

15. In this passage Motteville uses "elles," a feminine plural pronoun.

bonnes; mais si par malheur les moins parfaites y tombaient elles auraient du moins les maximes de Saint Paul [12] pour les défendre contre celles de votre sévérité, au lieu qu'étant convaincues d'une faiblesse qui passerait pour une espèce de crime dans vos Etats, elles et leurs Bergers seraient inconsolables de perdre en même temps votre estime, leur gloire et leur agréable patrie. Votre générosité en suivant mes conseils se trouverait soulagée de la peine que votre rigueur lui ferait souffrir en punissant les coupables, car il est à croire que vous n'auriez pas de facilité à faire du mal, au lieu que si vos sentiments l'emportent sur votre prudence, il serait à craindre que votre vertu ne fût trop souvent occupée à faire des malheureux[.] Je sais que je défends le parti de mes faibles et qu'il m'est honteux de soutenir ceux qui n'ayant point mon estime ne peuvent avoir de leur côté que ma seule pitié, mais dans un état bien policé il faut que le défectueux trouve sa subsistance et sa protection aussi bien que le plus parfait, c'est pourquoi je prends la liberté de vous représenter toutes ces raisons afin que ma compassion attire la vôtre, et que vous donniez des remèdes à tous les maux qui pourraient troubler le repos de vos sujets. A l'égard des autres Lois que vous leur donnez elles sont toutes belles, et pourvu qu'il s'en trouve, comme je n'en doute pas, d'assez vertueuses pour les observer, il n'y aurait rien de plus admirable que leur vie et leurs sentiments, mais comme je crois que leur nombre sera trop petit pour remplir votre Etat et qu'il vous en faudra souffrir de moins parfaits[,] je veux vous faire part d'une méditation que j'ai faite sur ce sujet afin de vous obliger à compter avec les faiblesses des hommes et à rendre grâces au Ciel de ce qu'il vous en a préservée. Quand nous naissons, ce qui premièrement occupe notre cœur c'est l'amitié et la tendresse que nous avons pour nos proches, pour ceux qui nous servent et pour les personnes de notre âge. Ces sentiments se conservent en quelques-uns et se perfectionnent par la raison et par l'usage de la vertu; cette vertu dans la suite des temps nous porte aux grandes choses, à l'observation des Lois divines et humaines, au culte de la Religion par où l'âme se connaît elle-même et voit que celui qui en est le Créateur est celui seul qui l'enrichit de ses dons; Elle nous porte aux belles connaissances, à s'acquitter dignement des devoirs où toutes les conditions de la vie nous engagent, et à chercher en toutes l'innocence et la justice. Voilà les véritables sages et les véritables heureux qui ne tombent point dans les dérèglements qui perdent tant de personnes et qui font tant de criminels et tant de misérables. Mais il est rare de trouver des hommes qui aient toujours été par un chemin si droit, et pour

---

12. Saint Paul, first letter to the Corinthians, 7: "To the unmarried and the widows I say that it is well for them to remain single as I do. But if they cannot exercise self-control, they should marry. For it is better to marry than to be aflame with passion."

defend them against your severe precepts: [16] instead of being convicted on account of a weakness that would be considered a sort of crime in your realm, they and their shepherds would be inconsolable because they would lose, all at once, your respect, their honor, and their agreeable homeland. If you follow my advice, your generosity would be relieved of the pain that your severity will cause if you punish the guilty, for it is hard to believe that you would find it easy to do harm. If, on the other hand, your feelings get the better of your wisdom, it might be feared that your virtue would be too often occupied in making people unhappy. I know that I am standing up for the weak and that it is shameful for me to defend those who, not having my respect, can only have my pity. In a well-regulated state, however, those who are somehow deficient must find sustenance and protection as much as the most perfect; this is why I take the liberty of presenting all these reasons to you, in the hope that my compassion will attract yours, and that you will provide cures for all the evils that could disturb the well-being of your subjects. As far as the other laws that you give them are concerned, they are all beautiful, and provided that there are some [women], as I do not doubt that there are, who are virtuous enough to observe them, there would be nothing more admirable than their life and their beliefs. Since, however, I think that their number will be too small to fill your state and that you will have to put up with some who are less than perfect, I want to share with you an observation that I made on this subject in order to make you realize how many weaknesses we all have and to make you give thanks to heaven that you have been saved from them. When we are born, our heart is first filled with the friendship and tenderness that we have for those close to us, for those who serve us, and for those who are the same age as we are. These feelings remain in some and are perfected through reason and the practice of virtue; over the course of time, this virtue leads us to great things, to the observance of divine and human laws, to the practice of religion by which the soul knows itself and sees that he who is its creator is the only one who enriches us with his gifts. It leads us to acquire the knowledge of noble things, to fulfill with dignity the duties that all the conditions of life require of us, and to seek out innocence and justice in every state. The true sages and the truly fortunate are those who do not succumb to the disorders that ruin so many people and produce so many criminals and wretches. But it is rare to find people who have always followed such a straight path, and usually from innocent youth

16. Saint Paul, first letter to the Corinthians, 7: "To the unmarried and the widows I say that it is well for them to remain single as I do. But if they cannot exercise self-control, they should marry. For it is better to marry than to be aflame with passion."

l'ordinaire de l'innocente jeunesse on passe [avec] les années à des passions violentes qui dominent l'âme et troublent le repos du cœur; c'est alors que l'on passe de l'amitié à l'amour, les uns à beaucoup de crimes qui se couvrent sous ce nom si familier et si doux de la galanterie: dans les Dames elle n'est pas toujours contraire à l'honnêteté, mais elle ne laisse pas d'être toujours fort blamable, et les autres qui paraissent plus sages à des engagements légitimes. Les premiers pour l'ordinaire conduisent les hommes et les femmes à beaucoup d'inquiétudes et de peines. Elles leur causent souvent des malheurs qui sont pour l'ordinaire suivis de leur perte. Les autres se lient à une condition fâcheuse qui pour être accompagnée d'innocence ne l'est pas toujours de bonheur. C'est ce dernier état qui fait dire sans doute qu'il est dur de changer l'amour en l'amitié; en effet quand l'âme a passé ce trajet qui mène de l'une à l'autre je suis assez persuadée de ce que vos vers nous enseignent, qu'elle ne saurait revenir à cette médiocrité,[13] et ne le pouvant je crois qu'en ce cas l'amour et l'amitié s'anéantissent entièrement, et qu'il ne reste souvent dans le mariage qu'une liaison d'habitude où l'intérêt a plus de part que la tendresse[.] Peu de personnes de celles qui ont laissé régner cette passion dans leur âme soit légitimement ou d'une autre manière peuvent demeurer longtemps exposées aux tourments qu'elle leur donne[:] la jalousie, les défauts des personnes qui s'aiment, et les perfidies dont on ne voit que trop d'exemples dans le monde usent enfin la patience et la sensibilité de ceux qui en souffrent, et il arrive quelquefois que ces fâcheuses expériences les rendent plus raisonnables plus sages et toujours plus indifférents. Je dis bien d'avantage que l'ingratitude que l'on rencontre dans le commerce de ces honnêtes gens qui ne le sont guère fait le même effet dans l'amitié. Nous savons par expérience qu'il n'y a quasi point de bonté dans les créatures, cette vérité qui nous est si connue nous dégoûte et fait que nous ne saurions plus jouir d'aucun plaisir dans la vie, mais il est plus rare de trouver des criminels dans l'amitié que dans l'amour, parce que la raison et l'innocence sont les ordinaires compagnes de l'amitié et que le dérèglement et la trahison sont naturellement celles de l'amour; c'est pourquoi je conviens avec vous, Grande Princesse, que pour rendre vos sujets heureux il faudrait qu'ils en demeurassent toujours à ce premier degré qui consiste seulement en la société des amis et je souhaiterais pour leur commodité que vous puissiez mettre des bornes à leurs sentiments pareilles à celles qui sont entre la France et l'Espagne. Je voudrais que comme la neige des Pyrénées refroidit les pays circonvoisins vous puissiez produire le même effet à l'égard de leurs désirs, et que ceux qui s'engagent dans les passions y trouvassent autant de difficultés que ces montagnes en

13. "Médiocrité" is used here in the sense of a balanced condition, without excess.

we move on over time to violent passions that dominate the soul and disrupt the heart's tranquillity. It is then that we make the transition from friendship to love. Some move on to the many offenses that disguise themselves behind the very sweet and familiar name of gallantry: in ladies, it is not always opposed to decency, but it is no less blamable. The others, who seem wiser, go on to contract legitimate engagements. The aforementioned offenses usually lead men and women into much pain and worry. They often cause misfortunes that usually lead to their ruin. The legitimate engagements are linked to an unfortunate situation, which, though accompanied by innocence, does not always bring happiness. It is this last state that must make people say that it is hard to change love into friendship; I am rather convinced of what your verses teach us, that indeed once the soul has taken the path that leads from the latter to the former, it cannot return to this less extreme state, and since it is not possible, I think that in such a case, love and friendship will both be entirely destroyed, and that often the only thing that remains in marriage is a relationship based on habit in which self-interest plays a greater role than tenderness. Few of those who have let this passion reign in their soul, legitimately or otherwise, can remain exposed to the torments that it produces for long: jealousy, the frailties of people in love, and the perfidy whose example we see only too frequently at the court, finally wear out the patience and sensibility of those who are afflicted by it, although it sometimes happens that these unfortunate experiences make them more reasonable, wiser— and always more indifferent. I would go even so far as to say that the ingratitude that one meets with when interacting with these supposedly honorable people has the same effect on friendship. We know from experience that there is almost no goodness in any creature: this truth, which we know only too well, disgusts us and makes it impossible for us to enjoy any pleasure in life. It is more rare, however, to find criminals in friendship than in love, because reason and innocence are the common companions of friendship, just as disorder and betrayal are the domain of love. This is why I agree with you, noble Princess, that for your subjects to be happy, they should always remain at this first stage, which consists only of the society of friends, and I wish that, for their convenience, you could create boundaries for their feelings similar to the ones between France and Spain. Just as the snow in the Pyrenees cools off the surrounding countries, I hope that you could produce the same effect on their desires, and that those who become involved with these passions would find as many difficulties in them as those mountains cause for travelers going from one kingdom to the other. Then, beautiful Princess, it would be easy to observe the wonderful laws that you give your subjects: they could be charming without falling into games of seduction;

font rencontrer aux voyageurs qui vont d'un Royaume à l'autre. Alors, Belle Princesse, il serait facile d'observer les belles Lois que vous donnez à vos sujets, ils pourraient avoir l'esprit galant sans tomber dans la galanterie, ils pourraient avoir cette politesse que vous leur ordonnez et qui est assurément la seule chose qu'il leur faut permettre, leur civilité n'aurait point d'autre objet que l'honnêteté et la bienséance et toutes choses seraient réglées selon l'ordre et la raison qui est seulement ce que vous voulez et que vos justes Lois ordonnent[.] Mais comme je compte toujours sur ce qui se pratique ordinairement plutôt que sur ce qu'il est quasi impossible de faire, que vous avez à commander à des hommes et non pas à des Anges[,] je vous dis encore une fois qu'il est à propos de permettre le mariage, si vous ne le faites il arrivera indubitablement que vos bergers abuseront de la permission que vous leur donnez, de l'esprit galant ils iront à la galanterie et sans y penser vous banniriez l'amour légitime pour introduire parmi eux le criminel. Il me souvient d'avoir lu autrefois un livre qui traitait de ces matières, son auteur estimait le mariage et lui donnoit beaucoup de louanges; pour moi je ne peux pas me résoudre d'en faire autant, je ne saurais aller contre mes sentiments et mon inclination, mais pour vous obliger à souffrir ce mal comme un remède à un plus grand, je voudrais à peu près me souvenir de ce qu'il dit en sa faveur. Il me semble qu'il allègue pour ses raisons que depuis la création du monde Dieu même l'a établi en la personne du premier homme, que les nations par lui trouvent leur durée et leur perpétuité, que le mariage doit être révéré comme celui qui règle la naissance et les biens de tous les hommes, qu'il établit l'ordre sur la terre et qu'il est le seul lien qui puisse engager l'homme et la femme à s'aimer avec innocence. Il fait plus, il maintient que l'amour est en général la source de toutes les vertus des hommes, il dit qu'il inspire la vaillance, qu'il fait aimer la gloire, et bien loin de la soumettre à l'ambition il croit que la plus belle et la plus louable vient de lui et que beaucoup de héros ont tout hasardé pour arriver à quelque grandeur que l'amour leur a fait désirer. Il nous représente toutes les femmes illustres qui ont sacrifié leur vie à l'amour légitime; il cite celle de Brutus et de Sénèque, et n'oublie pas celles qui se sont rendues célèbres par les larmes qu'elles ont repandues sur le tombeau de leurs maris. En effet, Grande Princesse, il faut avouer que dans notre siècle la douleur de Madame de Montmorency l'a rendue célèbre,[14] et même

---

14. Marie-Félice Orsini, duchesse de Montmorency (1600–1666). After her husband, Henri II, duc de Montmorency (1596–1632), was executed for lèse-majesté after having joined Montpensier's father, Gaston d'Orléans, in a conspiracy against Louis XIII, the duchesse did not remarry and remained in mourning for the rest of her life.

they could have the politeness that you expect of them and that is certainly the only thing that they should be permitted; their civility would have no object other than honor and decency, and everything would be modeled on order and reason, which is exactly what you want and what your just laws prescribe. As, however, I always expect the norm rather than what is almost impossible, and since you must rule over men and not angels, I tell you once again that it is appropriate to allow marriage: if you do not, your shepherds will certainly begin to take advantage of the license that you grant them; from courtesy, they will turn to gallantry and, without ever intending to, you would have banished legitimate love, only to introduce illicit love in its place. I remember having read some time ago a book about these matters: its author respected marriage and praised it a great deal. For my part, I cannot bring myself to go so far: I cannot go against my feelings and my inclination. Since, however, I would have you endure this ill as the lesser of two evils, I would like to recall more or less what he says in its favor. I believe that he cites as his reasons the fact that at the time of the creation of the world, God himself created it along with the first man, that nations use it to maintain their longevity and to perpetuate themselves, that marriage ought to be revered as the regulator of all men's birth and personal property, that it establishes order on earth, and that it is the only tie that can bind a man and a woman to love each other innocently. Furthermore, he maintains that love is, in general, the source of all of mankind's virtues; he says that it inspires valor, that it causes us to love glory, and, far from making it subservient to ambition, he believes that all that is most beautiful and most praiseworthy comes from love and that many heroes have risked everything to achieve some greatness because of love. He describes all the illustrious wives who sacrificed their lives for legitimate love; he cites those of Brutus and Seneca, and does not forget the women who became famous because of the tears they shed on their husbands' tombs. Indeed, noble Princess, we must admit that in our century, Madame de Montmorency's [17] sorrow made her famous, and one could even say that those ladies whom you mentioned and whom we have already discussed, Madame la marquise de Senecé and Madame la comtesse de Fleix, would not think it shameful to admit that they felt some small spark of that fire that is blameless when inclination and innocence are its cause: you your-

---

17. Marie-Félice Orsini, duchesse de Montmorency (1600–1666). After her husband, Henri II, duc de Montmorency (1596–1632), was executed for lèse-majesté after having joined Montpensier's father, Gaston d'Orléans, in a conspiracy against Louis XIII, the duchesse did not remarry and remained in mourning for the rest of her life.

on peut dire que ces Dames que vous m'avez citées et dont je vous ai déjà parlé Madame la Marquise de Senecé et Madame la Comtesse de Fleix ne tiendront point à honte d'avouer qu'elles ont senti quelque petite étincelle de ce feu qui n'est pas blâmable quand l'inclination avec l'innocence l'ont fait naître, et vous même les estimez de ce que le souvenir de cette affection les a empêchées de se remarier. Voilà mes sentiments particuliers, j'ose espérer que vous les estimerez, mais si mes conseils vous déplaisent, je vous promets, notre Illustre Souveraine, que je ferai mon possible pour aider à perfection- ner vos Bergères selon les lois que vous leur imposez. Je demeure d'accord que si elles peuvent subsister telles que vous les avez faites, elles contiennent plus de perfection et que ce serait une chose admirable si on pouvait bannir toute faiblesse de notre célèbre République.

LETTRE 5

Mademoiselle

à Madame de Motteville sur ce qu'elle pensait à se marier alors au Prince Charles de Lorraine l'année d'après que les Lettres précédentes avaient été écrites.

La tendresse de ma conscience ne me permet pas d'être sans remords quand je songe qu'après les beaux projets que nous fîmes l'année passée à Saint-Jean-de-Luz, j'en ai écouté de si différents et même de si opposés sans m'en entretenir avec vous. Hélas il est bien vrai que les années se suivent et qu'elles ne se ressemblent pas: j'ai souvent fait cette réflexion sur beaucoup de choses où je prenais intérêt, soit pour moi-même soit pour des personnes que j'aimais, maintenant l'état de ma fortune me donne plus d'occasion d'y penser que je n'ai fait, mais ces pensées sont plus propres à garder en moi- même qu'à communiquer aux autres. Tant qu'il n'est question que de traiter les chapitres en général on a cette pleine et chère liberté tant aimée de moi, mais quand on est sur le point de la perdre les avant-coureurs en effraient et l'ôtent quasi avant même qu'on l'ait perdue, la crainte de l'événement fait que je ne me sens pas libre de dire tout ce que je pense et tout ce que je sens; soyez pourtant assurée que je ne me dédirai jamais de ce que je vous ai écrit, je suis toujours dans les mêmes sentiments, mais les premiers devoirs ont sur moi- même un tel pouvoir qu'ils m'ôtent celui que j'ai sur moi-même, ainsi ils m'ont obligée d'écouter ce que je n'eusse jamais eu pensée ni dessein d'entendre. Le temps me mettra en état ou de continuer dans le dessein que nous avions fait, ou de me soumettre à la rude destinée qui m'expose à un autre sort, ou de le

self esteem them because the memory of their affection has prevented them from remarrying. Those are my own sentiments; I dare to hope that you will find some merit in them: if my advice displeases you, however, I promise you, our illustrious Sovereign, that I will do my utmost to help your shepherdesses improve themselves according to the laws that you lay down for them. I still agree that if these laws are able to prevail just as you conceived them, they contain more perfection and that it would be admirable if we could banish all weakness from our famous Republic.

LETTER 5

Mademoiselle

to Madame de Motteville containing her thoughts when she was considering marriage to Prince Charles of Lorraine the year after the preceding letters were written.

The tenderness of my conscience causes me remorse when I think about the lovely plans that we made last year at Saint-Jean-de-Luz: I have listened to such different and even conflicting ones without discussing them with you. Alas, it is only too true that the years pass and everything changes. I have often made this observation about many things in which I took an interest, both those that concerned me and those related to people I loved: now the state of my fortune gives me more opportunity to think about it than I ever have before, but these thoughts are better kept to myself than shared with others. So long as it is only a question of discussing these subjects in a general way, we enjoy that full and dear liberty that I love so much, but when we are about to lose our freedom, the early warning signals frighten it and take it away almost before it can be lost. The fear that that will happen makes me feel that I am not free to say all that I think and feel; nonetheless, rest assured that I will never go back on what I wrote you. I still feel the same way, but my first duties have such power over me that they take away that which I might have over myself: I am thus forced to listen to things that I never would have thought or intended to hear. Time will put me in a state either to continue with the plan that we made, or to submit myself to the harsh destiny that exposes me to another fate, or to defend our plan as forcefully as I can.

défendre du mieux qu'il me sera possible. L'incertitude où je me trouve du bien et du mal dont j'ai une parfaite connaissance me donne cet embarras, il me semble assez honnête pour vous le faire connaître, et il me semble que le silence dans une pareille conjoncture serait plus criminel que l'aveu de quelque chose qu'on pourrait dire de mal à propos, puisqu'une telle matière ne fournit rien; elle est la plus ingrate qu'on puisse choisir; c'est une terre plus pleine d'épines que de roses, et je crois que ces épines y piquent cruellement: c'est pourquoi il serait souhaitable que je ne fisse que la voir et que je m'en éloignasse autant que je parais en être proche, mais il faut craindre cette maudite étoile qui entraîne tout le monde cette année et le force à se soumettre aux tyranniques Lois de ce sacrement si ennemi de la liberté, je ne veux pas dire de la joie puisque j'en vois tant d'autres qui en ont beaucoup de s'être laissé captiver; mais je penserai tout ce qu'il me plaira et je vous donnerai toujours à connaître jusques à mon dernier moment tout ce que je croirai capable de vous confirmer dans la bonne opinion que vous avez conçue de moi et de ma fermeté dans mes bonnes résolutions. Priez Dieu que je n'imite pas ceux qui disent bien et qui font mal.

LETTRE 6

Madame de Motteville
à Mademoiselle

J'ai toujours cru, Belle Amelinte, que vous ne pourriez vous défendre de tomber dans cet honnête esclavage que l'Eglise honore du nom de sacrement. Cette puissance que les hommes se sont attribuée par une injuste usurpation paraîtrait trop faiblement établie s'il arrivait qu'une si belle proie leur échappât. Tout ce qu'il y a d'hommes au monde ont intérêt que ce noble orgueil qui vous les fait naturellement mépriser soit abattu par le triomphe de quelqu'un d'eux. Celui qui vous possédera, Eminente Princesse, sera trop heureux et sa gloire me déplaira par ce qu'en lui tous les autres se trouveront trop honorés. Je ne m'étonne donc pas si tant de vœux ont pu changer vos projets, car il est de l'ordre du ciel établi sur la terre que les causes particulières le cèdent au bien public. Votre embarras, vertueuse Amelinte, vous doit apporter de la gloire, et votre remords procède de votre innocence, vous avez raison d'en faire parade et de l'avouer librement, car si on osait mêler le ciel avec la terre on pourrait quasi dire de vous ce que ce grand Saint Jérome

The state of uncertainty in which I find myself about good and evil is, I know only too well, the cause of this state of confusion. I consider it reasonable enough to tell you about it, and feel that, in such circumstances, silence would be more criminal than confessing something that could be called inopportune. Because such a subject yields nothing, it is the most barren one that could be chosen: this land is filled more with thorns than roses, and I believe that those thorns prick mercilessly. This is why it would be desirable that, even though I may seem fixed on it, I should keep it in sight while getting as much distance from it as I can. I must fear, however, the inauspicious star that is carrying everyone along this year and forcing them to submit to the tyrannical laws of this sacrament that is so hostile to freedom, though I would not say to joy, since I see so many others who are very happy to have been enslaved. I will think, however, just what I wish, and I will always let you know up until my last moment, all that I deem capable of confirming your good opinion of me and of my steadfastness in my good intentions. Pray to God that I will not imitate those who advocate good deeds while performing bad ones.

LETTER 6

Madame de Motteville
to Mademoiselle

I always believed, beautiful Amelinte, that you could not prevent yourself from falling into the honorable slavery that the Church dignifies by calling it a sacrament. This authority that men have appropriated for themselves by unjust usurpation would seem too weakly implanted if such a beautiful prey escaped from them. All the men in the world have an interest in seeing this noble pride that makes you naturally despise them destroyed by the triumph of one of their number. He who possesses you, noble Princess, will be too happy and his glory will displease me because, in him, all men will find themselves honored. I am not surprised then that the wishes of so many were able to change your intentions, for it is heaven's order established here on earth that individual interests yield to the public good. Your confusion, virtuous Amelinte, should bring you glory, and your remorse is a product of your innocence: you are right to display it and to admit to it freely, for if we dared confuse heaven and earth, we could almost say of you what Saint

disait de Sainte Paule, que ses vices étaient les perfections des autres femmes.[15]
Nous vous avions choisie pour être la souveraine de nos déserts et de celles
qui en les habitant font profession d'estimer le Célibat. Il est bien juste que
vous ayez quelque honte de quitter notre parti et de faire céder votre inclination à la coutume, et à la violence que les hommes vous veulent faire en
vous engageant dans le leur. Ces sentiments que je vois en vous me font espérer de votre vertu que vous révérerez toujours nos Lois, que si vous êtes contrainte de ne les pas observer je m'assure du moins que vous leur donnerez
dans votre cœur le rang qu'elles méritent; ainsi nous ne laisserons pas de vivre
contentes dans l'espoir que nous aurons que la possession des sceptres et des
couronnes ne vous empêchera pas d'estimer et de protéger nos houlettes, vous
règnerez sur nous, Grande Princesse, avec la même puissance que si vous étiez
demeurée dans nos bois: nous nous consolerons de l'honneur que nous avons
eu de vous avoir pour notre Souveraine, le regret qui nous restera de vous avoir
perdue sera guéri par la pensée que nous aurons que les hommes, tant celui
qui vous possédera que ceux qui vous obéiront[,] ne douteront plus en vous
connaissant qu'il n'y ait des femmes qui les surpassent en mérite. Vous trou-
verez alors que nos déserts avaient des bornes trop petites pour enfermer en
elles une vertu aussi grande que la vôtre. Vous approuverez vous-même,
Généreuse Amelinte, les louanges que j'ai données au mariage. Vous trouve-
rez en considérant les avantages de ces deux conditions que puisque toutes
choses nécessairement sont mêlées de bien et de mal, il est bon en estimant
ce qui est meilleur de s'accommoder quand la raison le veut ainsi de ce qui
est le moins à notre goût. Nous ignorons pour l'ordinaire ce que nous devons
désirer pour être heureux, mais comme selon la philosophie chrétienne, et
même selon l'opinion de Sénèque[,] il n'y a rien qui puisse être appelé mal
que ce qui est contraire à la vertu, il nous faut marcher simplement sur cette
règle et vivre toujours vertueusement en toutes occasions, il n'importe quelle
profession de vie nous fassions pourvu que cette même vie soit bonne, juste
et raisonnable; ainsi vous devez être contente, et comme on peut juger de
l'avenir par le passé il est sans doute qu'en toutes les différentes conditions
que vous pourrez choisir vous y ferez toujours votre devoir. Je souhaite donc
que la gloire accompagne toutes vos actions, que l'équité règle toutes vos
passions et que la bonté les perfectionne, soit que vous commandiez à des
hommes en qualité de leur souveraine, comme une honnête femme, soit que
vous vous fassiez obéir par nos bergères comme une chaste Amazone que

---

15. Saint Paula (347–404) was a noble Roman woman. In the letter he wrote on the occasion
of her funeral, Saint Jerome says exactly what Motteville reports here.

Jerome said of Saint Paula, that her vices were other women's perfections.[18] We chose you to rule over our wilderness and over the women who, by living there, profess esteem for celibacy. You are right to be somewhat ashamed to have forsaken our cause and to have submitted your inclination to custom and to the violence that men want to do you by engaging you in their cause. These feelings that I see in you allow me to hope that, because of your virtue, you will always revere our laws: and that even if you are forced not to observe them, I am sure that, at least in your heart, you will give them the esteem they deserve; thus, we will continue to live content [19] in our hope that your scepters and crowns will not keep you from respecting and protecting our shepherds' staffs. You will reign over us, great Princess, with the same authority as if you had remained in our forest: we will console ourselves with the honor of having had you as our sovereign; the regret that will remain with us for having lost you will be assuaged by the thought that men, those who will obey you as well as he who will possess you, will, knowing you, no longer doubt that there are women whose merit surpasses theirs. Then you will see that the confines of our wilderness are too narrow to enclose a virtue as great as yours. You will yourself, generous Amelinte, approve of the compliments that I have given marriage. When you consider the advantages of those two states, you will find that, since all things are necessarily a mixture of good and bad, it is best to be satisfied with what is least to our liking when reason dictates it. We do not normally know what we should desire in order to be happy, but since, according to Christian philosophy, and even according to Seneca, nothing can be called evil except that which is contrary to virtue, we should simply continue to follow this rule and always behave virtuously in all situations. It does not matter what our state in life is as long as our life is good, just, and rational. You should, therefore, be content, and since the future can be judged by the past, in all the different states that you will choose, you will surely always do your duty. I hope then that glory will accompany all your actions, that reason will rule all your passions and that goodness will perfect them, and whether you command men as their sovereign, as an esteemed woman, or whether you command the obedience of our shepherdesses, as a chaste Amazon brought by her love of wisdom into our forest, that everywhere you will show that you possess all the qualities that should embellish the destiny of a great princess, and that in the

18. Saint Paula (347–404) was a noble Roman woman. In the letter he wrote on the occasion of her funeral, Saint Jerome says exactly what Motteville reports here.

19. In this passage all adjectives modifying "we" are feminine plural.

l'amour de la sagesse aurait transportée dans nos bois, que partout vous fassiez voir que vous avez toutes les qualités qui doivent orner la destinée d'une grande princesse et que dans l'avenir mon nom, comme je l'espère, puisse devenir célèbre par l'honneur que j'ai d'être

Votre très obéissante sujette
La Bergère Mélanie

LETTRE 7

Mademoiselle

à Madame de Motteville

de Forges ce premier d'août 1661 [16]

Après vous avoir parlé de l'inquiétude que me donnait le remords de ma conscience il est juste de vous faire savoir le repos dans lequel elle se trouve et la tranquillité dont je jouis maintenant. Enfin après trois mois de trouble et d'agitation je me trouve dans le calme d'une paix profonde et je demeure triomphante de tous les Ennemis qui me persécutaient. Assurément ce n'est pas la qualité qu'ils se donnent, et je leur devrais la justice de les nommer autrement; mais comme je ne me saurais contraindre et que je suis en possession de vous dire tout ce qui me vient dans la pensée[,] je les appelle ainsi puisqu'ils me voulaient captiver[.] Cependant admirez mon bonheur, celui qui devait être mon plus grand Ennemi et à qui de tout temps j'ai déclaré une guerre sans quartier redoute tellement mon pouvoir ou craint si fort tous les mauvais traitements qu'il a reçus de moi qu'au lieu de s'en venger dans cette occasion comme il l'aurait pu faire en suivant seulement la coutume qu'il a de se mêler toujours dans de pareilles choses, n'a fait aucun acte d'hostilité, au contraire il m'a servi comme s'il eût été à mes gages. Vous voyez par là quelle est son humeur, et sans doute vous la jugerez plus servile que généreuse, puisqu'il sert si bien ceux qui le maltraitent, et qu'il abandonne ceux qui se dévouent à lui, après cela je ne changerai pas d'avis. La vie qu'on mène en ce lieu a un peu de notre solitude, car rien n'est plus champêtre, mais la situation n'est pas telle que je la souhaite, non plus que la

---

16. Montpensier often took the waters at Forges-les-Eaux, a spa located near her estate at Eu, now in Seine-Maritime.

future my name will, I hope, become famous because of the honor that I have of being

Your very obedient subject,
The Shepherdess Mélanie

LETTER 7

Mademoiselle
to Madame de Motteville

Forges, the first of August 1661 [20]

Since I told you about the anxiety that my remorse was causing me, it is only right that I tell you about the repose in which my conscience now finds itself and the tranquillity I am enjoying. Finally after three months of turmoil and agitation, I find myself in the calm of a profound peace, and I have triumphed over all the enemies who were persecuting me. To be sure, that is not the name they give themselves, and I should rightly call them by another name. Since I cannot restrain myself, however, and because I am bound to tell you everything that comes to mind, I name them thus because they wanted to imprison me. Nevertheless, admire my felicity: he who should have been my greatest enemy and against whom from time immemorial I have declared war with no quarter granted so dreads my power, or is so afraid of all the bad treatment he has received from me, that rather than revenging himself on this occasion, as he could have done just by following his habit of always interfering in such things, he did not commit any act of hostility: on the contrary, he has served me as if he were in my pay. You see by this what his humor is, and certainly you will think it more servile than generous, since he serves those who mistreat him so well and abandons those who devote themselves to him: henceforth, I will not change my opinion. The life that we lead in this place does have a little of our solitude, for nothing is more pastoral, but the situation is not exactly how I would like it to be, no more than

20. Montpensier often took the waters at Forges-les-Eaux, a spa located near her estate at Eu, now in Seine-Maritime.

compagnie que le hasard forme plutôt que le choix. Il serait difficile de pouvoir donner ici de ces louanges que je promets à nos solitaires et qui ne doivent point passer la bonne santé, peu de personnes ayant le teint d'une fraîcheur et d'une vivacité à les en faire louer sans cajolerie, aussi est-on quasi tous les jours dans les remèdes, et l'usage des Eaux en est un. On donne au jeu le reste du temps, pour moi je ne m'y applique pas fort, je fais presque ce que je ferais si nous étions déjà dans notre retraite, je lis et je travaille à mon ouvrage, je cause le matin avec tout le monde qui va à la fontaine, et l'après-dinée je reçois des visites pour vivre avec les vivants bien qu'il y en ait ici qui avec raison pourraient n'être point estimés vivants pour nous, puisqu'il faut être plus sain de corps et d'esprit qu'ils ne sont. Il y en a pourtant qui ne doivent pas être confondus avec les autres et qui méritent place dans quelqu'une de nos cabanes; ce sont ceux que je vois le plus souvent et avec qui j'ai le plus de conversation; mais je passe mes plus agréables heures à rêver à notre dessein, à louer Dieu de ce que les obstacles qui s'y pouvaient opposer par le passé sont enfin levés et ne m'en laissent point prévoir à l'avenir. Je me trouve comme ces petits oiseaux qui ont été longtemps en cage qui sont si aises de voler où il leur plaît et de n'avoir plus que les champs et les bois pour prison. Je respire l'air avec un plaisir nonpareil quand je songe que c'est avec une pleine et entière liberté et que je me vois quasi pour jamais hors d'état de la perdre, je crois devoir dire quasi, par ce que je trouve encore ma vie trop longue pour dire rien de plus positif, et même mon humeur que je confesse un peu contrariante me fait parler de la sorte de crainte de faire plaisir à quelques-uns, car il y a des gens assez ennemis du mérite et de ceux qui le possèdent pour être bien aise de les voir sortir du monde. Il ne faut donc plus leur donner cette joie jusqu'à ce que nous soyons en état d'en goûter une plus parfaite dans notre solitude, alors nous ne nous soucions guère ni de leurs discours ni de leurs sentiments. Mais avant que de finir j'aurais quelque envie de vous gronder un peu de la dernière réponse que vous m'avez faite, vous me parlez sur ce chapitre comme si j'eusse déjà été assez malheureuse pour n'en pouvoir plus sortir et qu'il eût fallu m'en plaindre et m'en consoler ainsi que d'une chose sans remède. Non Dieu merci je n'en étais pas là et je me trouve à l'épreuve d'une plus grande extrémité que celle où je me suis vue réduite.

is my company, formed more by chance than by choice. It would be hard for me to give here the kind of praise that I guarantee our recluses, praise that should not go beyond good health. Few people here have a complexion that is fresh and lively enough for it to be praised without flattery, which is why we are almost always trying cures, taking the waters being one such. We spend the rest of our time playing cards and games; for my part, I do not devote much energy to this. I do almost exactly what I would do if we were already in our retreat: I read and I work at my needlework; I converse each morning with all the people who go to the fountain,[21] and after dinner I receive visits in order to live with the living, even though there are some here who rightly would not seem to us to be alive, since we would expect them to be more sound in body and mind than they are. Nonetheless, there are some who should be distinguished from the others and who deserve a place in one of our huts; they are the ones whom I see most often and with whom I converse most regularly. My most agreeable hours, however, are spent dreaming about our plan and thanking God that the obstacles that could have stood in its way in the past have finally been removed, with no signs of new ones ahead. I find myself like those little birds who have been in a cage for a long time and who are so overjoyed to fly wherever they like and to have only the fields and the woods for a prison. I breathe the air with incomparable pleasure when I think that I do so with full and complete freedom and that I see almost no possibility of ever losing it. I believe I must say "almost," because I have too much life still to live to say anything more definite, and even my temperament, which I confess is a little perverse, makes me speak this way for fear of pleasing certain individuals, for there are those who so hate merit and those who possess it that they are truly pleased to see them distance themselves from the court. We should not give them this pleasure until we are in a position to enjoy a more perfect one in our solitude, at which time we will be completely indifferent to what they say and what they think. But before I finish, I would like to scold you a bit for your last response to me: you speak to me on this matter as if I were already so unfortunate that I could no longer get out of the situation and as if you already had to pity me and console me as you would if things were irreversible. No, thank God, I am not there yet and I find myself confronted by a greater extremity than that to which I have seen myself reduced.

---

21. Those who went for thermal cures brought their cups to fountains where mineral waters were dispensed.

LETTRE 8

Madame de Motteville

à Mademoiselle

Je m'étais soumise à souffrir que votre destinée fût pareille à celle de beaucoup de femmes illustres, mais je vois bien que votre vertu, qui en effet est extraordinaire, vous défend de marcher par la voie commune. Je rends grâces au ciel, sage Amelinte, de ce que vous vous êtes échappée des pièges que les hommes vous ont tendus. Votre bonheur et leur infortune me donne de la joie, et je trouve que nous sommes fort obligées à votre fierté de ce qu'elle a puni leur audace. Triomphez donc, Grande Princesse, et vengez-nous toutes de ces Ennemis audacieux qui en général font profession de nous mépriser et dont les plus sages quand il s'agit des grandes choses disent souvent que les femmes n'en sont pas capables; comme il y a eu parmi eux des Rois et des Souverains qui ont eu assez de lumière et de raison pour former des désirs pour vous, il faut les en louer à mesure de leurs souhaits et penser pour votre satisfaction qu'il est encore plus beau ce me semble de régner par vous-même et sur vous-même que de vous assujettir à leur puissance par celle que l'ambition pourrait avoir sur vous. Votre exemple sera sans doute suivi des plus illustres de notre sexe. J'espère que les hommes demeureront seuls dans les villes, et que nos déserts se rempliront de tout ce qu'il y a de meilleur et de plus précieux sur la terre. Ces lois si belles, si pures et si estimables que vous avez faites, en les observant nous rendront heureuses. Nous y trouverons le repos et le bonheur qu'on ne rencontre point ailleurs, et si tout de bon nous étions sages nous ferions que tous ces vains discours deviendraient une très véritable histoire. En attendant que cela puisse être je fais, Amelinte, ces souhaits en votre faveur.

> Puisse la main divine à jamais vous bénir
> Et la publique voix des siècles à venir
> Etre un jour dans nos bois l'Echo de vos louanges.[17]

---

17. In the manuscript's margin, the author of these lines is identified as "Bertaut, évêque de Séez." Jean Bertaut (1552–1661), bishop of Séez in Savoy and a minor poet, was Motteville's uncle.

LETTER 8

Madame de Motteville
to Mademoiselle

I forced myself to accept that you would share the fate of many illustrious women, but I see clearly that your virtue, which is indeed extraordinary, forbids you from following the common path. I give thanks to the heavens, wise Amelinte, that you have escaped the snares that men had laid for you. Your happiness and their misfortune give me joy, and I find that we are very much obliged[22] to your pride for having punished their audacity. Rejoice then, noble Princess, and avenge us all[23] against these audacious enemies who generally profess to despise us: even the wisest among them, when the subject of great deeds comes up, often say that women are incapable of them. Since among them there have been kings and sovereigns who were enlightened and rational enough to desire you, they must be praised in proportion to their desires and we must think, for your satisfaction, that it is more wonderful to reign by yourself and over yourself than to subject yourself to their authority because of the power ambition could have over you. Your example will certainly be followed by the most illustrious members of our sex. I hope that men will remain alone in the cities and that our desert will be full of all that is best and most precious on earth. Our obedience to the laws that you have made—so beautiful, so pure, and so estimable—will make us happy. In them, we will find the peace and the happiness that cannot be encountered elsewhere and, if we were truly wise, we would turn all these vain speeches into a very true story. While waiting for this to come to pass, I make, Amelinte, these wishes for you:

> Let the divine hand bless you forever
> And let public opinion in the centuries to come
> One day in our forest be the echo of your praises.[24]

22. Feminine plural in French.

23. She uses "toutes," feminine plural.

24. In the manuscript's margin, the author of these lines is identified as "Bertaut, bishop of Séez." Jean Bertaut (1552–1661), bishop of Séez in Savoy and a minor poet, was Motteville's uncle.

VOLUME EDITOR'S
BIBLIOGRAPHY

PRIMARY SOURCES

Montpensier, Anne-Marie-Louise d'Orléans, duchesse de. *Lettres de Mademoiselle de Montpensier, de Mesdames de Motteville et de Montmorenci et de Mademoiselle du Pré, et de Madame la Marquise de Lambert.* Paris: Léopold Collin, 1806.

———. *Mémoires.* Ed. Christian Bouyer. 2 vols. Paris: Librairie Fontaine, 1985.

———. *Mémoires.* Ed. Adolphe Chéruel. 4 vols. Paris: G. Charpentier, 1858–59.

———. *Mémoires.* Ed. Claude Petitot. 4 vols. Paris: Foucault, 1824–25.

———. *Portraits littéraires.* Ed. Christian Bouyer. Paris: Séguier, 2000.

———. *Recueil de quelques pièces nouvelles et galantes, tant en prose qu'en vers.* Cologne: Pierre du Marteau, 1667. (First edition of the first four letters of her correspondence with Motteville.)

Motteville, Françoise Bertaut, dame de. *Mémoires pour servir à l'histoire d'Anne d'Autriche, épouse de Louis XIII, roi de France.* Ed. Claude Petitot. 5 vols. Paris: Foucault, 1824–25.

Saliez, Antoinette de Salvan, comtesse de. *Lettres de Mesdames de Scudéry, de Salvan de Saliez, et de Mlle Descartes.* Paris: Léopold Collin, 1806.

Scudéry, Madeleine de. *Artamène, ou Le Grand Cyrus.* 1649–53. 10 vols. Geneva: Editions Slatkine, 1973.

———. *Clélie, histoire romaine.* 1654–60. 10 vols. Geneva: Editions Slatkine, 1973.

SECONDARY SOURCES

Beasley, Faith. *Revising Memory: Women's Fiction and Memoirs in Seventeenth-Century France.* New Brunswick: Rutgers University Press, 1990.

Bertaud, Madeleine. "En Marge de leurs *Mémoires,* une correspondance entre Mlle de Montpensier and Mme de Motteville." *Travaux de littérature* 3 (1990): 277–95.

Bouyer, Christian. *La Grande Mademoiselle: Anne-Marie-Louise d'Orléans duchesse de Montpensier.* Paris: A. Michel, 1986.

Chartier, Roger. *Publishing Drama in Early Modern Europe.* London: British Museum, 1999.

Cherbuliez, Juliette. "Before and Beyond Versailles: The Counter-Court of the Duchesse de Montpensier, 1652–1660." *Nottingham French Studies* (September 2000): 129–39.

Cholakian, Patricia Francis. "Mademoiselle de Montpensier." In *Women and the Politics of Self-Representation in Seventeenth-Century France.* Newark: University of Delaware Press, 2000.

DeJean, Joan. *Ancients Against Moderns: Culture Wars and the Making of a Fin de Siècle.* Chicago: University of Chicago Press, 1997.

———. *Tender Geographies: Women and the Origins of the Novel in France.* New York: Columbia University Press, 1991.

Garapon, Jean. *La Grande Mademoiselle mémoraliste: Une Autobiographie dans le temps.* Geneva: Droz, 1989.

Hill, Christopher. *Milton and the English Revolution.* New York: Viking, 1978.

Lougee, Carolyn. *Le Paradis des femmes: Women, Salons, and Social Stratification in Seventeenth-Century France.* Princeton: Princeton University Press, 1976.

Pitts, Vincent. *La Grande Mademoiselle at the Court of France, 1627–1693.* Baltimore: Johns Hopkins University Press, 2000.

Sackville-West, Vita. *Daughter of France: The Life of La Grande Mademoiselle.* Garden City, N.Y.: Doubleday, 1959.

Stanton, Domna. "The Ideal of 'repos' in Seventeenth-Century French Literature." *L'Esprit créateur* 15, nos. 1–2 (spring–summer 1975): 79–104.

Tristan L'Hermite, François. *Œuvres complètes,* ed. Bernard Bray. Vol. 1. Paris: Honoré Champion, 1999.

Williams, Raymond. *The Country and the City.* London: Chatto and Windus, 1973.

Woolf, Virginia. *A Room of One's Own.* 1929. New York: Harcourt Brace Jovanovich, 1957.

SERIES EDITORS'
BIBLIOGRAPHY

PRIMARY SOURCES

Alberti, Leon Battista (1404–72). *The Family in Renaissance Florence*. Trans. Renée Neu Watkins. Columbia: University of South Carolina Press, 1969.

Arenal, Electa, and Stacey Schlau, eds. *Untold Sisters: Hispanic Nuns in Their Own Works*. Trans. Amanda Powell. Albuquerque: University of New Mexico Press, 1989.

Astell, Mary (1666–1731). *The First English Feminist: Reflections on Marriage and Other Writings*. Ed. and introd. Bridget Hill. New York: St. Martin's Press, 1986.

Atherton, Margaret, ed. *Women Philosophers of the Early Modern Period*. Indianapolis: Hackett, 1994.

Aughterson, Kate, ed. *Renaissance Woman: Constructions of Femininity in England: A Source Book*. London: Routledge, 1995.

Barbaro, Francesco (1390–1454). *On Wifely Duties*. Trans. Benjamin Kohl in *The Earthly Republic*, ed. B. Kohl and R. G. Witt, 179–228. Philadelphia: University of Pennsylvania Press, 1978. Translation of the preface and book 2.

Behn, Aphra. *The Works of Aphra Behn*. 7 vols. Ed. Janet Todd. Columbus: Ohio State University Press, 1992–96.

Boccaccio, Giovanni (1313–1375). *Famous Women*. Ed. and trans. Virginia Brown. The I Tatti Renaissance Library. Cambridge: Harvard University Press, 2001.

———. *Corbaccio or the Labyrinth of Love*. Trans. Anthony K. Cassell. 2nd rev. ed. Binghamton, N.Y.: Medieval and Renaissance Texts and Studies, 1993.

Bruni, Leonardo (1370–1444). "On the Study of Literature (1405) to Lady Battista Malatesta of Moltefeltro." In *The Humanism of Leonardo Bruni: Selected Texts*. Trans. and introd. Gordon Griffiths, James Hankins, and David Thompson, 240–51. Binghamton, N.Y.: Medieval and Renaissance Studies and Texts, 1987.

Castiglione, Baldassare (1478–1529). *The Book of the Courtier*. Trans. George Bull. New York: Penguin, 1967.

Cerasano, S. P., and Marion Wynne-Davies, eds. *Readings in Renaissance Women's Drama: Criticism, History, and Performance 1594–1998*. London: Routledge, 1998.

Christine de Pizan (1365–1431). *The Book of the City of Ladies*. Trans. Earl Jeffrey Richards. Foreword Marina Warner. New York: Persea Books, 1982.

———. *The Treasure of the City of Ladies*. Trans. Sarah Lawson. New York: Viking Penguin, 1985. Also trans. and introd. Charity Cannon Willard. Ed. and introd. Madeleine P. Cosman. New York: Persea Books, 1989.

Crawford, Patricia, and Laura Gowing, eds. *Women's Worlds in Seventeenth-Century England: A Source Book.* London: Routledge, 2000.

Elizabeth I: Collected Works. Ed. Leah S. Marcus, Janel Mueller, and Mary Beth Rose. Chicago: University of Chicago Press, 2000.

Elyot, Thomas (1490–1546). *Defence of Good Women: The Feminist Controversy of the Renaissance.* Facsimile Reproductions. Ed. Diane Bornstein. New York: Delmar, 1980.

Erasmus, Desiderius (1467–1536). *Erasmus on Women.* Ed. Erika Rummel. Toronto: University of Toronto Press, 1996.

Ferguson, Moira, ed. *First Feminists: British Women Writers 1578–1799.* Bloomington: Indiana University Press, 1985.

Glückel of Hameln (1646–1724). *The Memoirs of Glückel of Hameln.* Trans. Marvin Lowenthal. New introd. Robert Rosen. New York: Schocken Books, 1977.

Henderson, Katherine Usher, and Barbara F. McManus, eds. *Half Humankind: Contexts and Texts of the Controversy about Women in England, 1540–1640.* Urbana: University of Illinois Press, 1985.

Joscelin, Elizabeth. *The Mother's Legacy to Her Unborn Childe.* Ed. Jean D. LeDrew Metcalfe. Toronto: University of Toronto Press, 2000.

Kaminsky, Amy Katz, ed. *Water Lilies, Flores del agua: An Anthology of Spanish Women Writers from the Fifteenth through the Nineteenth Century.* Minneapolis: University of Minnesota Press, 1996.

Kempe, Margery (1373–1439). *The Book of Margery Kempe.* Trans. Barry Windeatt. New York: Viking Penguin, 1986.

King, Margaret L., and Albert Rabil Jr., eds. *Her Immaculate Hand: Selected Works by and about the Women Humanists of Quattrocento Italy.* Binghamton, N.Y.: Medieval and Renaissance Texts and Studies, 1983; 2nd rev. paperback ed., 1991.

Klein, Joan Larsen, ed. *Daughters, Wives, and Widows: Writings by Men about Women and Marriage in England, 1500–1640.* Urbana: University of Illinois Press, 1992.

Knox, John (1505–1572). *The Political Writings of John Knox: The First Blast of the Trumpet against the Monstrous Regiment of Women and Other Selected Works.* Ed. Marvin A. Breslow. Washington: Folger Shakespeare Library, 1985.

Kors, Alan C., and Edward Peters, eds. *Witchcraft in Europe, 400–1700: A Documentary History.* Philadelphia: University of Pennsylvania Press, 2000.

Krämer, Heinrich, and Jacob Sprenger. *Malleus Maleficarum* (ca. 1487). Trans. Montague Summers. London: Pushkin Press, 1928. Reprint, New York: Dover, 1971.

Larsen, Anne R., and Colette H. Winn, eds. *Writings by Pre-Revolutionary French Women: From Marie de France to Elizabeth Vigée-Le Brun.* New York: Garland, 2000.

Lorris, William de, and Jean de Meun. *The Romance of the Rose.* Trans. Charles Dahlbert. Princeton: Princeton University Press, 1971; Reprint, University Press of New England, 1983.

Marguerite d'Angoulême, Queen of Navarre (1492–1549). *The Heptameron.* Trans. P. A. Chilton. New York: Viking Penguin, 1984.

Russell, Rinaldina, ed. *Sister Maria Celeste's Letters to Her Father, Galileo.* San Jose: Writers Club Press, 2000.

Teresa of Avila, Saint (1515–1582). *The Life of Saint Teresa of Avila by Herself.* Trans. J. M. Cohen. New York: Viking Penguin, 1957.

Weyer, Johann (1515–1588). *Witches, Devils, and Doctors in the Renaissance: Johann Weyer,*

De praestigiis daemonum. Trans. John Shea. Ed. George Mora with Benjamin G. Kohl, Erik Midelfort, and Helen Bacon. Binghamton, N.Y.: Medieval and Renaissance Texts and Studies, 1991.

Wilson, Katharina M., ed. *Medieval Women Writers.* Athens: University of Georgia Press, 1984.

———, ed. *Women Writers of the Renaissance and Reformation.* Athens: University of Georgia Press, 1987.

Wilson, Katharina M., and Frank J. Warnke, eds. *Women Writers of the Seventeenth Century.* Athens: University of Georgia Press, 1989.

Wollstonecraft, Mary. *A Vindication of the Rights of Men and a Vindication of the Rights of Women.* Ed. Sylvana Tomaselli. Cambridge: Cambridge University Press, 1995. Also *The Vindications of the Rights of Men, The Rights of Women.* Ed. D. L. Macdonald and Kathleen Scherf. Peterborough, Ontario: Broadview Press, 1997.

Women Critics 1660–1820: An Anthology. Ed. Folger Collective on Early Women Critics. Bloomington: Indiana University Press, 1995.

Women Writers in English 1350–1850: fifteen published through 1999 (projected thirty-volume series suspended). Oxford University Press.

Woolf, Virginia. *A Room of One's Own.* 1929. New York: Harcourt Brace & Co., 1957.

Wroth, Lady Mary. *The Countess of Montgomery's Urania.* 2 parts. Ed. Josephine A. Roberts. Tempe: MRTS, 1995, 1999.

———. *The Poems of Lady Mary Wroth.* Ed. Josephine A. Roberts. Baton Rouge: Louisiana State University Press, 1983.

Zayas Maria de. *The Disenchantments of Love.* Trans. H. Patsy Boyer. Albany: State University of New York Press, 1997.

———. *The Enchantments of Love: Amorous and Exemplary Novels.* Trans. H. Patsy Boyer. Berkeley: University of California Press, 1990.

SECONDARY SOURCES

Akkerman, Tjitske, and Siep Sturman, eds. *Feminist Thought in European History, 1400–2000.* London: Routledge, 1997.

Barash, Carol. *English Women's Poetry, 1649–1714: Politics, Community, and Linguistic Authority.* New York: Oxford University Press, 1996.

Battigelli, Anna. *Margaret Cavendish and the Exiles of the Mind.* Lexington: University of Kentucky Press, 1998.

Beilin, Elaine V. *Redeeming Eve: Women Writers of the English Renaissance.* Princeton: Princeton University Press, 1987.

Benson, Pamela Joseph. *The Invention of Renaissance Woman: The Challenge of Female Independence in the Literature and Thought of Italy and England.* University Park: Pennsylvania State University Press, 1992.

Blain, Virginia, Isobel Grundy, and Patricia Clements, eds. *The Feminist Companion to Literature in English: Women Writers from the Middle Ages to the Present.* New Haven: Yale University Press, 1990.

Bloch, R. Howard. *Medieval Misogyny and the Invention of Western Romantic Love.* Chicago: University of Chicago Press, 1991.

Bornstein, Daniel, and Roberto Rusconi, eds. *Women and Religion in Medieval and Renaissance Italy.* Trans. Margery J. Schneider. Chicago: University of Chicago Press, 1996.

Brant, Clare, and Diane Purkiss, eds. *Women, Texts and Histories, 1575–1760.* London: Routledge, 1992.

Briggs, Robin. *Witches and Neighbours: The Social and Cultural Context of European Witchcraft.* New York: HarperCollins, 1995; Viking Penguin, 1996.

Brown, Judith C. *Immodest Acts: The Life of a Lesbian Nun in Renaissance Italy.* New York: Oxford University Press, 1986.

Cervigni, Dino S., ed. *Women Mystic Writers. Annali d'Italianistica* 13 (1995) (entire issue).

Cervigni, Dino S., and Rebecca West, eds. *Women's Voices in Italian Literature. Annali d'Italianistica* 7 (1989) (entire issue).

Charlton, Kenneth. *Women, Religion and Education in Early Modern England.* London: Routledge, 1999.

Chartier, Roger. *Publishing Drama in Early Modern Europe.* London: British Library, 1999.

Chojnacka, Monica. *Working Women in Early Modern Venice.* Baltimore: Johns Hopkins University Press, 2001.

Chojnacki, Stanley. *Women and Men in Renaissance Venice: Twelve Essays on Patrician Society.* Baltimore: Johns Hopkins University Press, 2000.

Cholakian, Patricia Francis. *Rape and Writing in the Heptameron of Marguerite de Navarre.* Carbondale: Southern Illinois University Press, 1991.

Davis, Natalie Zemon. *Society and Culture in Early Modern France.* Stanford: Stanford University Press, 1975. Especially chapters 3 and 5.

———. *Women on the Margins: Three Seventeenth-Century Lives.* Cambridge: Harvard University Press, 1995.

De Erauso, Catalina. *Lieutenant Nun: Memoir of a Basque Transvestite in the New World.* Trans. Michele Ttepto and Gabriel Stepto; foreword Marjorie Garber. Boston: Beacon Press, 1995.

Dixon, Laurinda S. *Perilous Chastity: Women and Illness in Pre-Enlightenment Art and Medicine.* Ithaca: Cornell University Press, 1995.

Dolan, Frances, E. *Whores of Babylon: Catholicism, Gender and Seventeenth-Century Print Culture.* Ithaca: Cornell University Press, 1999.

Donovan, Josephine. *Women and the Rise of the Novel, 1405–1726.* New York: St. Martin's Press, 1999.

Erickson, Amy Louise. *Women and Property in Early Modern England.* London: Routledge, 1993.

Ezell, Margaret J. M. *Writing Women's Literary History.* Baltimore: Johns Hopkins University Press, 1993.

Ferguson, Margaret W., Maureen Quilligan, and Nancy J. Vickers, eds. *Rewriting the Renaissance: The Discourses of Sexual Difference in Early Modern Europe.* Chicago: University of Chicago Press, 1987.

Fletcher, Anthony. *Gender, Sex and Subordination in England 1500–1800.* New Haven: Yale University Press, 1995.

Frye, Susan, and Karen Robertson, eds. *Maids and Mistresses, Cousins and Queens: Women's Alliances in Early Modern England.* Oxford: Oxford University Press, 1999.

Gallagher, Catherine. *Nobody's Story: The Vanishing Acts of Women Writers in the Marketplace, 1670–1820.* Berkeley: University of California Press, 1994.

Gelbart, Nina Rattner. *The King's Midwife: A History and Mystery of Madame du Coudray.* Berkeley: University of California Press, 1998.

Goldberg, Jonathan. *Desiring Women Writing: English Renaissance Examples.* Stanford: Stanford University Press, 1997.

Goldsmith, Elizabeth C. *Exclusive Conversations: The Art of Interaction in Seventeenth-Century France.* Philadelphia: University of Pennsylvania Press, 1988.

Goldsmith, Elizabeth C., ed. *Writing the Female Voice.* Boston: Northeastern University Press, 1989.

Goldsmith, Elizabeth C., and Dena Goodman, eds. *Going Public: Women and Publishing in Early Modern France.* Ithaca: Cornell University Press, 1995.

Greer, Margaret Rich. *Maria de Zayas.* University Park: Pennsylvania State University Press, 2000.

Hall, Kim F. *Things of Darkness: Economies of Race and Gender in Early Modern England.* Ithaca: Cornell University Press, 1995.

Hampton, Timothy. *Literature and the Nation in the Sixteenth Century: Inventing Renaissance France.* Ithaca: Cornell University Press, 2001.

Hardwick, Julie. *The Practice of Patriarchy: Gender and the Politics of Household Authority in Early Modern France.* University Park: Pennsylvania State University Press, 1998.

Haselkorn, Anne M., and Betty Travitsky, eds. *The Renaissance Englishwoman in Print: Counterbalancing the Canon.* Amherst: University of Massachusetts Press, 1990.

Herlihy, David. "Did Women Have a Renaissance? A Reconsideration." *Medievalia et Humanistica,* NS 13 (1985): 1–22.

Hill, Bridget. *The Republican Virago: The Life and Times of Catharine Macaulay, Historian.* New York: Oxford University Press, 1992.

Hill, Christopher. *Milton and the English Revolution.* New York: Viking, 1978.

A History of Women in the West. Volume 1: *From Ancient Goddesses to Christian Saints.* Ed. Pauline Schmitt Pantel. Cambridge: Harvard University Press, 1992. Volume 2: *Silences of the Middle Ages.* Ed. Christiane Klapisch-Zuber. Cambridge: Harvard University Press, 1992. Volume 3: *Renaissance and Enlightenment Paradoxes.* Ed. Natalie Zemon Davis and Arlette Farge. Cambridge: Harvard University Press, 1993.

Horowitz, Maryanne Cline. "Aristotle and Women." *Journal of the History of Biology* 9 (1976): 183–213.

Hufton, Olwen H. *The Prospect Before Her: A History of Women in Western Europe, 1: 1500–1800.* New York: HarperCollins, 1996.

Hull, Suzanne W. *Chaste, Silent, and Obedient: English Books for Women, 1475–1640.* San Marino, Calif.: Huntington Library, 1982.

Hutner, Heidi, ed. *Rereading Aphra Behn: History, Theory, and Criticism.* Charlottesville: University Press of Virginia, 1993.

Hutson, Lorna, ed. *Feminism and Renaissance Studies.* New York: Oxford University Press, 1999.

James, Susan E. *Kateryn Parr: The Making of a Queen.* Aldershot: Ashgate Publishing, 1999.

Jankowski, Theodora A. *Women in Power in the Early Modern Drama.* Urbana: University of Illinois Press, 1992.

Jed, Stephanie H. *Chaste Thinking: The Rape of Lucretia and the Birth of Humanism.* Bloomington: Indiana University Press, 1989.

Jordan, Constance. *Renaissance Feminism: Literary Texts and Political Models*. Ithaca: Cornell University Press, 1990.

Kelly, Joan. "Did Women Have a Renaissance?" In *Women, History, and Theory*. Chicago: University of Chicago Press, 1984. Also in *Becoming Visible: Women in European History*, ed. Renate Bridenthal, Claudia Koonz, and Susan M. Stuard. 3rd ed. Boston: Houghton Mifflin, 1998.

———. "Early Feminist Theory and the *Querelle des Femmes*." In *Women, History, and Theory*. Chicago: University of Chicago Press, 1984.

Kelso, Ruth. *Doctrine for the Lady of the Renaissance*. Foreword Katharine M. Rogers. Urbana: University of Illinois Press, 1956, 1978.

King, Carole. *Renaissance Women Patrons: Wives and Widows in Italy, c. 1300–1550*. New York: St. Martin's Press, 1998.

King, Margaret L. *Women of the Renaissance*. Foreword Catharine R. Stimpson. Chicago: University of Chicago Press, 1991.

Krontiris, Tina. *Oppositional Voices: Women as Writers and Translators of Literature in the English Renaissance*. London: Routledge, 1992.

Kuehn, Thomas. *Law, Family, and Women: Toward a Legal Anthropology of Renaissance Italy*. Chicago: University of Chicago Press, 1991.

Kunze, Bonnelyn Young. *Margaret Fell and the Rise of Quakerism*. Stanford: Stanford University Press, 1994.

Labalme, Patricia A., ed. *Beyond Their Sex: Learned Women of the European Past*. New York: New York University Press, 1980.

Laqueur, Thomas. *Making Sex: Body and Gender from the Greeks to Freud*. Cambridge: Harvard University Press, 1990.

Larsen, Anne R., and Colette H. Winn, eds. *Renaissance Women Writers: French Texts/American Contexts*. Detroit: Wayne State University Press, 1994.

Lerner, Gerda. *The Creation of Patriarchy* and *Creation of Feminist Consciousness, 1000–1870*. (Two-volume history of women.) New York: Oxford University Press, 1986, 1994.

Levin, Carole, and Jeanie Watson, eds. *Ambiguous Realities: Women in the Middle Ages and Renaissance*. Detroit: Wayne State University Press, 1987.

Levin, Carole, et al. *Extraordinary Women of the Medieval and Renaissance World: A Biographical Dictionary*. Westport, Conn.: Greenwood Press, 2000.

Lindsey, Karen. *Divorced Beheaded Survived: A Feminist Reinterpretation of the Wives of Henry VIII*. Reading, Mass.: Addison-Wesley, 1995.

Lochrie, Karma. *Margery Kempe and Translations of the Flesh*. Philadelphia: University of Pennsylvania Press, 1992.

MacCarthy, Bridget G. *The Female Pen: Women Writers and Novelists 1621–1818*. Preface Janet Todd. New York: New York University Press, 1994. (Originally published by Cork University Press, 1946–47).

Maclean, Ian. *The Renaissance Notion of Woman: A Study of the Fortunes of Scholasticism and Medical Science in European Intellectual Life*. Cambridge: Cambridge University Press, 1980.

———. *Woman Triumphant: Feminism in French Literature, 1610–1652*. Oxford: Clarendon Press, 1977.

Matter, E. Ann, and John Coakley, eds. *Creative Women in Medieval and Early Modern Italy*. Philadelphia: University of Pennsylvania Press, 1994. (Sequel to the Monson collection, below.)

Mendelson, Sara, and Patricia Crawford. *Women in Early Modern England, 1550–1720.* Oxford: Clarendon Press, 1998.

Monson, Craig A., ed. *The Crannied Wall: Women, Religion, and the Arts in Early Modern Europe.* Ann Arbor: University of Michigan Press, 1992.

Newman, Karen. *Fashioning Femininity and English Renaissance Drama.* Chicago: University of Chicago Press, 1991.

Okin, Susan Moller. *Women in Western Political Thought.* Princeton: Princeton University Press, 1979.

Ozment, Steven. *The Bürgermeister's Daughter: Scandal in a Sixteenth-Century German Town.* New York: St. Martin's Press, 1995.

Pacheco, Anita, ed. *Early [English] Women Writers: 1600–1720.* New York: Longman, 1998.

Pagels, Elaine. *Adam, Eve, and the Serpent.* New York: HarperCollins, 1988.

Panizza, Letizia, ed. *Women in Italian Renaissance Culture and Society.* Oxford: European Humanities Research Centre, 2000.

Panizza, Letizia, and Sharon Wood, eds. *A History of Women's Writing in Italy.* Cambridge: Cambridge University Press, 2000.

Perry, Ruth. *The Celebrated Mary Astell: An Early English Feminist.* Chicago: University of Chicago Press, 1986.

Raven, James, Helen Small, and Naomi Tadmor, eds. *The Practice and Representation of Reading in England.* Cambridge: Cambridge University Press, 1996.

Richardson, Brian. *Printing, Writers and Readers in Renaissance Italy.* Cambridge: Cambridge University Press, 1999.

Riddle, John M. *Contraception and Abortion from the Ancient World to the Renaissance.* Cambridge: Harvard University Press, 1992.

———. *Eve's Herbs: A History of Contraception and Abortion in the West.* Cambridge: Harvard University Press, 1997.

Rose, Mary Beth, ed. *Women in the Middle Ages and the Renaissance: Literary and Historical Perspectives.* Syracuse: Syracuse University Press, 1986.

Rosenthal, Margaret F. *The Honest Courtesan: Veronica Franco, Citizen and Writer in Sixteenth-Century Venice.* Foreword Catharine R. Stimpson. Chicago: University of Chicago Press, 1992.

Schiebinger, Londa. *The Mind Has No Sex?: Women in the Origins of Modern Science.* Cambridge: Harvard University Press, 1991.

———. *Nature's Body: Gender in the Making of Modern Science.* Boston: Beacon Press, 1993.

Shemek, Deanna. *Ladies Errant: Wayward Women and Social Order in Early Modern Italy.* Durham, N.C.: Duke University Press, 1998.

Sobel, Dava. *Galileo's Daughter: A Historical Memoir of Science, Faith, and Love.* New York: Penguin Books, 2000.

Sommerville, Margaret R. *Sex and Subjection: Attitudes to Women in Early-Modern Society.* London: Arnold, 1995.

Spencer, Jane. *The Rise of the Woman Novelist: From Aphra Behn to Jane Austen.* Oxford: Basil Blackwell, 1986.

Spender, Dale. *Mothers of the Novel: 100 Good Women Writers Before Jane Austen.* London: Routledge, 1986.

Sperling, Jutta Gisela. *Convents and the Body Politic in Late Renaissance Venice.* Foreword Catharine R. Stimpson. Chicago: University of Chicago Press, 1999.

Steinbrügge, Lieselotte. *The Moral Sex: Woman's Nature in the French Enlightenment.* Trans. Pamela E. Selwyn. New York: Oxford University Press, 1995.

Stuard, Susan M. "The Dominion of Gender: Women's Fortunes in the High Middle Ages." In *Becoming Visible: Women in European History,* ed. Renate Bridenthal, Claudia Koonz, and Susan M. Stuard. 3rd ed. Boston: Houghton Mifflin, 1998.

Summit, Jennifer. *Lost Property: The Woman Writer and English Literary History, 1380–1589.* Chicago: University of Chicago Press, 2000.

Teague, Frances. *Bathsua Makin, Woman of Learning.* Lewisburg, Pa.: Bucknell University Press, 1999.

Todd, Janet. *The Secret Life of Aphra Behn.* London, New York: Pandora, 2000.

———. *The Sign of Angelica: Women, Writing and Fiction, 1660–1800.* New York: Columbia University Press, 1989.

Walsh, William T. *St. Teresa of Avila: A Biography.* Rockford, Ill.: TAN Books, 1987.

Warner, Marina. *Alone of All Her Sex: The Myth and Cult of the Virgin Mary.* New York: Knopf, 1976.

Warnicke, Retha M. *The Marrying of Anne of Cleves: Royal Protocol in Tudor England.* Cambridge: Cambridge University Press, 2000.

Watt, Diane. *Secretaries of God: Women Prophets in Late Medieval and Early Modern England.* Cambridge: D. S. Brewer, 1997.

Welles, Marcia L. *Persephone's Girdle: Narratives of Rape in Seventeenth-Century Spanish Literature.* Nashville: Vanderbilt University Press, 2000.

Whitehead, Barbara J., ed. *Women's Education in Early Modern Europe: A History, 1500–1800.* New York: Garland, 1999.

Wiesner, Merry E. *Women and Gender in Early Modern Europe.* Cambridge: Cambridge University Press, 1993.

Willard, Charity Cannon. *Christine de Pizan: Her Life and Works.* New York: Persea Books, 1984.

Williams, Raymond. *The Country and the City.* New York: Oxford University Press, 1973.

Wilson, Katharina, ed. *An Encyclopedia of Continental Women Writers.* New York: Garland, 1991.

Woodbridge, Linda. *Women and the English Renaissance: Literature and the Nature of Womankind, 1540–1620.* Urbana: University of Illinois Press, 1984.

Woods, Susanne. *Lanyer: A Renaissance Woman Poet.* New York: Oxford University Press, 1999.

Woods, Susanne, and Margaret P. Hannay, eds. *Teaching Tudor and Stuart Women Writers.* New York: MLA, 2000.

INDEX